THE
LAWS
OF
ETERNITY

IRH PRESS

BOOKS
IRH PRESS
New York

ISBN: 978-1-958655-16-0
Cover Image: Vector Tradition/pixta.jp
fuwapuka/pixta.jp

Printed in Canada

First Edition

THE
LAWS
OF
ETERNITY

EL CANTARE UNVEILS
THE STRUCTURE OF
THE SPIRIT WORLD

RYUHO OKAWA

IRH PRESS

Contents

CHAPTER ONE

The World of the Fourth Dimension

CHAPTER TWO

The World of the Fifth Dimension

The World of the Sixth Dimension

CHAPTER FOUR
The World of the Seventh Dimension

The World of the Eighth Dimension

CHAPTER SIX

The World of the Ninth Dimension

Afterword

Preface

The title of this book, *The Laws of Eternity*, is exactly what this book is about. The Eternal Truth that has never been preached before, and will never be preached again, is condensed logically into this single book.

The three distinctive pillars of the Laws of El Cantare are as follows: the vast structure of the Laws that encompasses all aspects of life's Truths; the theory of time that describes the historical roles of tathagatas and bodhisattvas from a long-term perspective that spans several thousands of years; and the theory of space that fully explains the multidimensional structure of the Real World, the world of the hereafter. Following the books, *The Laws of the Sun* (the structure of the Laws) and *The Golden Laws* (the theory of time), I wrote this book to disclose the theory of space and complete the Trilogy of the basic Laws. By reading them, the framework of the Laws of El Cantare should become apparent to you.

Now, the eternal mysteries have been revealed. The ultimate secrets of Earth Spirit Group, which were under the veil called legends and myths, have been disclosed. I send this book to the world with the wholehearted wish that all world religions will overcome their differences and be united as one.

Ryuho Okawa
Master & CEO of Happy Science Group
July, 1997

CHAPTER ONE

The World of
the Fourth Dimension

1

The Other World and This World

Where did we come from and where will we go after we die?

For us human beings, this is a vital question that always lingers at the depths of our minds. However, very few people have been able to give a clear answer. This is because it is impossible to answer it without clarifying the relationship between the other world and this world. Unfortunately, in the current academic fields on earth, there are not enough academic achievements or established methods to clearly explain this.

One way to get a slight idea is through the activities of the spiritual mediums that have appeared in every age. However, there are many kinds of spiritual mediums. Although some can be trusted, most of them are mentally immature or have strange personalities. For this reason, people cannot generally believe what they say. Even if they tell you, for example, "I can see the spirit of Mr. So-and-so" or "In a year, you will end up like this," there is no way to prove it. So you can hardly believe their words and will only grow anxious.

Put simply, when we try to reveal the truth about the relationship between the other world and this world, we are left with an uncertain feeling because we cannot experience and verify what spiritual mediums claim to have experienced.

If we could all share the experiences that they have, everyone would believe that the other world exists. But sadly, in reality, only those with special abilities can experience the other world. That is why people in general cannot be sure that the other world exists. As a result, people with worldly common sense do not want to acknowledge the existence of the other world or the relationship between the other world and this world.

It is human nature to always ponder the meaning of life or the purpose of life. These are essential matters in life and unless we grasp what kind of existence we are from the perspective of the Great Universe, we cannot fully establish the meaning or purpose of our life.

If, as materialists say, human life begins all of a sudden in a mother's womb, continues for 60 to 70 years, and ends after the person is cremated or buried, then we should live with a way of thinking that accords with this life view. However, religious leaders teach that there is another world called the Real World, and souls are born from the Real World into this world to live a life of several decades for soul training. And even after "graduating" from this world, souls keep striving to improve themselves further in the Real World. If this is the truth, then we must adopt a different way of thinking.

Let's say that life is like a school education. There are several ways of looking at it, but how materialists view life is like saying that compulsory education is over after we finish six years of elementary school. To them, life is no more than elementary school days and it ends there. On the other hand, those who believe in the Spirit World and that human beings go through reincarnations while living eternal lives, have a view that sees life as a continuous course of education. It is the same as thinking that after graduating from elementary school, you move on to junior and senior high school, university, graduate school, and then continue learning various things even after you start working. If we compare these two perspectives on life, it is obvious which one will better contribute to human evolution and improvement. When we believe that humans are aiming to evolve eternally, we will be able to improve much more significantly.

If we believe that we only live once and that humans are like ephemeral sparklers who live for just a brief period of time, we will not be able to find great significance or purpose in life. To burn our short lives to the fullest like sparklers, we will indulge ourselves in various kinds of pleasure, be swept away by desires for material things, and live as we like with no restraints. Everyone would live for themselves only. If life was just about living for several decades, it would only be natural to feel that we cannot waste our time and should enjoy ourselves instead. However, if life is eternal, our efforts to do something for others will eventually come back around as nourishment for our souls.

So it is extremely important to understand the perspective of the other world and this world when considering the meaning of life or the purpose and mission of life. Without it, we cannot understand the real meaning of life or what human beings really are.

2

The World after Death

Let me call the place where humans go after leaving this world—after casting away their physical bodies—*another world* or *the other world*. What kind of world is it? What kind of world awaits those who have left this world?

Because people living in this world do not know what is waiting for them after death, they get anxious and fearful and say, "I don't want to die." These words reveal an attachment to earthly life. In reality, 99 percent of people will most probably say that they do not want to die. They say this not only because they find life in this world comfortable, but also because they are anxious and afraid of the other world, the world after death. In some cases, however, people find this world very hard or too unbearable to live in. Their suffering in this world surpasses their anxiety and fear of death and they choose to leave for the other world prematurely by taking their own lives.

Either way, I think ignorance of the other world, or the world after death, is at the root of these ways of thinking. People have a hard time because the study of the other world has yet to be established as a field in the academic world. That is why I believe that I need to explain the world after death as clearly as possible and fulfill my mission as a "marine pilot." Setting out to sea without a nautical map makes for an uneasy voyage, but if you have a detailed map, you will not feel so anxious. If you know where you have come from and where you are going, or what continent your ship is heading toward, that is, if you understand the nautical map well, you will have a safe journey.

So, what actually happens to humans when they leave their physical bodies? Let me talk about this.

In many of my books, I have described that life is not just about the few decades spent in a physical body but that it carries over from this world to the next. Yet, human beings still resist death when they are faced with it. Those suffering from illness say they do not want to die, and doctors make every effort to prolong their lives. However, when viewed from the other world, a dying person's guardian spirit, guiding spirit, or other angels have already come to him or her. They have already started preparing to guide the person whose death is drawing near.

After the person takes their last breath, their spiritual body leaves their physical body. At first, the person does not recognize what is happening to them and feels as if there are two people—one lying on the bed and the other moving freely. When the one who is moving freely talks to other people, they are ignored. They can also pass through walls and other material objects. At first, they find these experiences astounding.

The soul of the dead person continues to hover around their physical body thinking, "That is me lying on the bed," but they will be truly shocked when their body is taken to the crematorium to be cremated. Not knowing what to do, the soul will float around the crematorium thinking, "What kind of life awaits me from here?" The soul will feel a strong sense of anxiety about the life that awaits them because no one told them about it.

It is at this point that their guardian spirit appears and begins to persuade them to return to the other world. However, if the soul has lived decades on earth without believing in the existence of the other world, it will not be easily convinced. So their guardian spirit stays on earth and tries to persuade them for several weeks. As we can see from the Buddhist memorial services that are conducted on the seventh day and forty-ninth day after a person's death, the souls of the dead are usually allowed to remain on earth for 20 to 30 days after death. During this period, souls, in general, will go back to heaven after being convinced by their guardian and guiding spirits.

However, the souls of those who have a very strong attachment to something in this world, such as their children, father, mother, wife, husband, land, house, property, company, or business will not want to leave this world. These souls will become what are known as "earthbound spirits" and continue to wander around on earth. They are what we call "ghosts" in this world. They are beings who have yet to awaken as spirits.

3

Memories of a Physical Body

When souls arrive in the other world, most of them are shocked and bewildered, but in time, they get used to living there. They gradually realize that they can live without a physical body. They are surprised to know that they can survive without eating or drinking, for example, for 20 or 30 days. They also realize that people living on earth cannot hear them even if they talk to them. That is when they come to understand that they should not be so hung up on this world.

These people who have now become spirits will then acquire new senses: spiritual senses. They can also float in the air, pass through material objects, and travel long distances in an instant. If they still have concerns about life on earth and wish to say goodbye to a relative or see a friend one last time, their spiritual bodies travel hundreds of miles the moment they think of doing so. At first, these experiences bring them fresh excitement, but they eventually become usual occurrences to them. Then, they start considering how they should live in this new world. They start exploring new ways of seeing the world and recognizing themselves, similar to what first graders go through in elementary school. As they live there, the memories of their lives on earth would gradually fade away, but some spirits find that the memories grow much stronger. This means spirits will be distinguished into these two types.

In most cases, spirits who have been wandering around in this Phenomenal World after death will eventually be led to a "reception center" in the fourth dimension, guided by their deceased friends or parents, or by their guardian spirits. There, they have to reflect on their lives on earth. The spiritual point of view would be the standard of their self-reflection; they reflect on how mistakenly they lived from a spiritual perspective. In other words, spirits are made to deeply reflect on how they lived their lives believing that they are only physical bodies.

Spirits who find through self-reflection that their life on earth was very much based on their physical body and that they did not awaken to their spiritual nature, will go to the so-called "hell" in the fourth dimension of their own volition. They will go through severe trials there. But those who honestly admit their mistakes and repent for failing to lead a spiritual life on earth will go to the Fairy Realm—also located in the fourth dimension—where spirits who live in harmony reside.

Therefore, where spirits go in the afterlife depends on the memories they have of their lives when they still had physical bodies. It is not Enma, or King Yama, who will pass judgment; it is their own conscience, good heart, or true nature as children of Buddha that will make the judgment.

In other words, they, themselves, are aware of the need for further spiritual discipline. So they choose to train themselves in hell at their own discretion after consulting with their guardian spirits. However, as they spend a long time in hell, they forget about the choice they made and begin thinking they are being forced to live under harsh conditions.

On the other hand, the truly vicious spirits will not go through this process but will go straight to hell immediately after death. These spirits are in a rage trying to delude people on earth. They are undoubtedly similar in nature to the gangsters and *yakuza* of this world.

4

The Activities of Angels

Perhaps, those who are believed to be the "people with common sense" of today cannot easily believe in the existence of angels. Even devout Christians may not truly believe that they are real, although they may think it in their heads. Christians talk of "the Father, the Son, and the Holy Spirit," but while they can somewhat understand God the Father and Christ the Son, they seem to have little idea about the Holy Spirit.

Over 90 percent of people think of angels and devils as beings that only appear in fairy tales such as *Grimm's Fairy Tales*. They can hardly believe that these figures actually exist in the 20th century and laugh them off instead. But angels and devils are not beings that only appear in folk tales. Throughout history, both in the East and West, there have always been stories about angel-like beings and devil-like beings. This is true in both advanced and developing countries. This is because these beings really exist.

In a nutshell, an "angel" is a generic term for high spirits, but there are differences in their levels. I will explain this further later on, but there are angels living in the upper level of the sixth dimensional Light Realm. They are generally called *shoten zenshin* [lit. various gods and deities]. Spirits at the bodhisattva and tathagata levels are also called angels.

Angels at the initial level of their training are responsible for saving the souls of people who have just left the earthly world. These angels are working to save human souls in a more practical way, rather than by preaching the Laws. There are hundreds of millions of such angels. They guide the souls who have just left this world for the other world or provide various kinds of education at the "reception center." What is more, they go and guide each soul according to his or her ideology, beliefs, and religious circumstances. In Christian countries, Christianity-related angels provide guidance, whereas in Buddhist countries, Buddhism-related bodhisattvas mostly take on this role. In other words, they appear before each soul in a way that the soul—the one who is receiving guidance—will find easy to believe.

Having said this, however, angels are not just living in the other world. Many of them are reborn on earth every few hundred to a thousand years. Why do they do this? One reason is to undergo their own soul training, and another is to purify the earthly world. But these are not all the reasons; they are also born from time to time so as not to forget how it feels to live as a human. If they remain in the other world for too long, they will lose their sense of how humans in this world think and feel. To become better educators, they, too, need to know how it feels to live on earth. So angels are also born into this world out of necessity. By acquiring earthly senses, they are able to preach in a way that is suited to each person and to guide more and more people.

So the first thing humans perceive after death is the activities of angels. Souls who are emitting brilliant light will come to them. These bright souls appear as angels with wings before Christians, as Buddhist monks before Buddhists, and as Shinto priests before Shinto believers. All of the angels and high spirits are shining brightly and their halo will be emitting brilliant light. On seeing their presence, even those who did not believe in God or Buddha feel the urge to put their hands together in prayer and say, "O Buddha," or "O God." This is because it is human instinct to believe in the existence of high spirits, Buddha, and God.

5

A New Departure

Guided by these angels, humans who have left the earth will gradually become ready to make a new departure. By "a new departure," I mean a brand-new experience.

Of course, we all made a new departure when we were born. All spirits—be they high spirits or undeveloped spirits—experienced a new departure when they were conceived in their mother's womb and were born into this world. They started their lives from scratch.

The brand-new experience I am talking about refers to this: after living several decades in this world and graduating from the school called "earth," spirits enter a new school. In this new journey, they encounter new teachers, find new textbooks, and learn new lessons. In this way, spirits who have returned to the fourth dimension are taught extensively what it is like to be spiritual.

They are taught many things by angels or their old friends and teachers who have returned to the other world ahead of them and gradually realize that they will set off on a new journey. These things provide them with important guiding principles for their new lives in the Spirit World, although in most cases, they forget these principles once they settle down in their new lives. Nevertheless, they are taught many things as guidance when they first arrive in the Spirit World.

At this stage, some spirits have to make a new departure to hell. But to all of you living on earth, please understand clearly that hell is not a place that is equal in size to heaven. I must make this point very clear.

If we call this earthly world the third dimension, hell is only a small part of the other world that stretches from the fourth dimension to the ninth, tenth, and even higher dimensions. Hell is just a den of negative thought energy that is in one corner of the fourth dimension and is in no way equal in size to heaven. Please keep this in mind.

There are many different kinds of people on earth, but there are no such species as "sick people." Some people get sick and that is why there are hospitals. In the same way, in the other world, spirits whose minds are ill are training in hell and undergoing rehabilitation. It is very important that you see them in this way. They are sick and are suffering from problems in their minds, but they are also trying hard to gain lessons in hell in their own way.

You can provide healthy people with various kinds of guidance; you can teach them how to drive a car, ride a bicycle, run a long or short-distance race, or do jumps. However, you cannot guide sick people in the same way.

Sick people need to start by learning how to walk with crutches or with someone supporting them by the arm. In hell, they need this kind of practice first.

In contrast, those who enter the Fairy Realm see various kinds of beings that they never saw on earth. They encounter, for example, creatures that appear in old tales and legends. While we do not see dragons or *kappa* (Japanese river imps) in this world, these creatures exist in the other world, and we can actually see them. We can also see small fairy-like beings flying around flower gardens. Many kinds of mysterious spiritual beings live in the other world, and by witnessing these creatures, souls further develop their spiritual senses to understand the new world.

6

The True Nature of Spirits

Now, let me go on to talk about the true nature of spirits. As I have just explained, it is not easy for humans to become familiar with their spiritual nature shortly after they have left their physical bodies. It is hard to acquire spiritual senses soon after death. For example, while they are still alive, humans can reach out and grab any object, but once they become a spirit wandering near the third dimensional earthly world, they cannot take hold of anything. Facing this fact, they all think, "I can't believe this." But before long, they begin to see these new senses as normal, regardless of whether they are aware that they have become spirits or not. Then, eventually, they decide for themselves whether to move on to heaven or hell.

When deciding whether to go to heaven or hell, the most vital factor is whether you know who you really are. In other words, it is whether or not you know your true nature. This will determine the kind of life you will lead in the other world.

Even if some people do not believe in the spiritual world, they have most probably seen images or heard stories about the other world from picture books, old tales, or novels. They just did not realize how much truth these stories told.

What kind of life will lead you to heaven and what kind of life will lead you to hell? Nowadays, very few people or places can give a clear answer to this question. Even people who believe in the existence of the other world cannot tell whether their ways of living, from a spiritual viewpoint, are appropriate for heaven or hell.

The simplest way to tell is to refer to religious commandments or precepts to see if certain actions are sinful or not. You can then conclude that those who committed many sins will fall to hell whereas those with few sins will go to heaven. This way of thinking has been popular since ancient times. For the last few thousand years of human history, this type of thinking has been common in both the East and West, regardless of race. A few famous examples of religious precepts that have been applied this way are the Ten Commandments of Moses and, before that, the Code of Hammurabi in Mesopotamia.

In modern society, we have many laws, and laws ultimately come from the Laws taught by the light of guiding spirits. Because it was impossible to explain the Laws in an easy-to-understand way, they were sometimes taught in the form of precepts such as, "You may do this, but you must not do that." So, for the majority of people, including those who know about the spiritual world, the simplest checkpoint is to see if they are living in a way that goes against those precepts.

This makes it easier for them to think about whether they will go to heaven or hell.

Precepts are, indeed, easy to understand in that they distinguish what is right and what is wrong in a simple way. The most typical one is "Do not kill," which implies that if you kill someone you will go to hell, and if you do not, you will go to heaven. Another example is "Do not steal," meaning if you steal things you will go to hell, and if you do not, you will go to heaven. This way, you can have a dichotomic way of thinking when considering right and wrong. We cannot dismiss precepts altogether as childish ideas, because there is some truth shining in them as well.

Nevertheless, it is not precepts that truly determine whether you will go to heaven or hell. In the end, people who have awakened to their true nature as children of Buddha through their 60 to 70 years of life on earth are the ones who are in heaven. What is more, the more they manifested their true nature, the higher the realm they reached in the heavenly world. On the other hand, those who did not realize their true nature and failed to live as a child of Buddha while on earth are now undergoing severe trials in hell. This is the truth about the afterlife.

7

The Unknown

I have said that hell exists in the spiritual world. You may have heard about hell from folktales, but if you actually find yourself there, you will be absolutely shocked. As you may have heard, there are various types of hell and you also find beings like ogres and devils there. I am sure that everyone would be shocked if they actually saw these places and beings with their own eyes. There are ogre-like beings 10 to 13 feet tall, and even some hellish spirits that chase after you with swords.

In the Hell of Lust, human spirits writhe in agony in a pond of blood. In the Hell of Hungry Ghosts, many are suffering and crying out in hunger, "Give me food. I want to eat." They are skin and bones like the farmers from long ago who starved to death during a famine.

The Hell of Beasts also exists. There, human spirits no longer take on a human form. Creatures with the body of a horse, ox, or pig but with a human face really do exist there, as the Japanese writer Ryunosuke Akutagawa depicted in a novel about humans who fell to the Hell of Beasts. Some spirits have become large snake-like creatures and are slithering around on the ground in hell.

Spirits in the Hell of Beasts do not understand why they became the way they are, but it is because they do not understand the true nature of spirits. The world of spirits is a place where your thoughts become reality.

When these people were alive, they did not know that what they thought in their minds had already manifested in the world of the mind. So they lived thinking they could live in any way they wanted because no one could see what was in their minds. If their minds were transparent and all their thoughts could be seen by others while they were still alive, they would have been too ashamed to appear in public. People who lived with such embarrassing thoughts will be shocked to find that once they return to the other world or the world of spirits, everything in their minds can be seen by others, and their appearance will change to conform to their thoughts.

While people are alive, if their bodies change into snakes whenever they have envious or resentful thoughts, they would quickly realize that their thoughts are wrong. But because this does not happen under the laws of the third dimension, people remain unaware of their wrong thoughts. In the other world, however, what you think manifests instantly. For example, those who are obsessed with someone of the opposite sex will fall to the Hell of Lust, where they will keep chasing after the opposite sex. Those who always think of deceiving others will turn into fox-like spirits in the other world, while those who persistently envy or resent others will turn into snake-like spirits. Human spirits can take on other animal-like appearances as well.

Human spirits that turn into animal-like spirits will try to temporarily escape hell to get away from the agonies there and possess people on earth. But they cannot possess just anyone; they can only possess people who are creating hell in their minds. Living people hold many kinds of thoughts and create various kinds of spiritual worlds within their minds, and those who create hell in their minds can fall prey to the spirits of hell.

People who create a hell of lust in their minds will be visited by spirits from the Hell of Lust, whereas people who create a hell of animals or hell of beasts in their minds will be visited by animal-like spirits. People who create an abysmal hell in their minds, that is to say, people who hold distorted philosophies or religious thoughts and make others go astray, will be possessed by religious leaders or philosophers who have fallen to the Abysmal Hell.

After all, hell exists in the world of the mind, that is, in people's thoughts. The spirits of hell can possess living people because they have hell in their minds. It is the hell in people's minds that hellish spirits will sneak into. That is how this mystical world works. You all need to know this.

8

Eternal Life

There is a phrase that the spirits suffering in hell always say: "I would rather die than continue living in this form." Some of them curse Buddha and God in every possible way, saying, "If I have to live as a snake I wish God had just killed me," whereas others say, "It would have been better if God had killed me rather than leaving me to struggle in a sea of blood in the Hell of Lust." Those who have fallen to the Abysmal Hell and are living alone in complete darkness, living in the desert, or confined to a cave are saying, "If this is the kind of life that awaited me, I wish God had just taken my life altogether."

With my spiritual sight, I have seen many so-called religious leaders who have fallen to the Abysmal Hell and are suffering all alone in very deep darkness or very deep swamps. They were regarded as great religious leaders and admired in many ways while they were alive. Among them are also many founders of religious groups that are now led by second or third-generation leaders. These founders wonder why they, of all people, are in a place like that when they guided tens of thousands or millions of believers in the earthly world. They are all saying, "I would rather have had my life taken than come to a place like this." They say this because they do not know what their future holds; they have no idea how much longer they have to suffer in a pitch-black world.

Souls live forever. Souls have eternal life. This is the greatest blessing for souls who led a harmonious life on earth with beautiful hearts and returned to heaven after death; they can continue to live in a wonderful place. However, for people who have fallen to hell, having eternal life in itself is a punishment. If their life ended altogether after death, they would not need to continue suffering in hell. But there is no end to the life of a soul. This very fact is punishing to them.

If people knew about the nature of the true world, they would surely understand that to think or do evil during their life in this world does not pay. But because they do not believe in eternal life and instead think that life ends with death, they do whatever they want and try to attain a higher position even if it means hurting others or kicking others out of their positions. If they knew that living in such a way would only cause them to fall to hell and thrash about in eternal agony instead of enjoying eternal life, they would surely realize that a way of life like that does not pay off at all.

On the other hand, if people knew that a life of modest goodness would lead to a blissful life or the most wonderful life in the other world, they would surely regret not having done more good while they were alive. One act of goodness in this world is worth about ten acts of goodness in the other world. Living in this world is truly difficult; souls are undergoing spiritual training while being "blindfolded." So, leading a heavenly life in this world, where we need to find our way in the darkness, is a spiritual training that is worth five or ten times that in the other world.

Those who have lived in a heavenly way for several decades in this world will find that their deeds will be rewarded tenfold in the other world. The earthly world is such a precious world. However, the many bad acts that you commit in this world by thinking, "It shouldn't be a problem to do this," will also come back to you fivefold or tenfold. Such a harsh reality awaits us.

Some people may think that they should do good because they will be praised, or they should not do evil because it is wrong. But if you really want to cherish yourself, you will find that you cannot do evil but can only do good. Once you have acquired the right views of life and the right views of the world, you will only be able to live in such a way. No one wants to do anything that does not pay off.

Especially, people who will end up in hell hate to do this. They are doing things that are disadvantageous to themselves because they do not know the consequences. Therefore, we must let them know about this as soon as possible.

9

Memories of Past Lives

I have talked about many things regarding heaven and hell, but what is most surprising upon returning to the fourth dimension is that we recall the memories of our past lives. This is the most peculiar and surprising experience for spirits who have returned to the other world.

When we are alive, we are satisfied with the life experiences we have—we are born as a baby, we study through kindergarten, elementary school, junior and senior high school, and university, then become adults and eventually age. But when we return to the other world, we find that our true life experience is not limited to such a short span of time. Furthermore, our true life does not just span thousands or tens of thousands of years or even millions of years. It is much, much longer.

In fact, your souls have a history of tens of millions or even hundreds of millions of years. Upon returning to the other world, the memories of your past lives will come back to you, and you will learn that you have been living as a human being for a long, long time.

But the spirits in hell can hardly recall the memories of their past lives. Life in hell is very agonizing and harsh, and so it is difficult for them to look back on their past while they go through so much suffering. For example, when you are agonizing over a severe toothache, it is not easy for you to think about your past or reflect on it even if you are told to do so. In the same way, although the spirits agonizing in hell have the ability to recall the memories of their past lives, it is practically impossible for them to do so.

On the other hand, spirits who have returned to heaven will start recalling their past lives, although the extent to which they can remember depends on each spirit. Spirits who led an ordinary life in this world will vaguely recall just one or two immediate past lives upon returning to the other world. They simply remember having done something a long, long time ago. But as they advance to higher levels, they will be able to recall the memories of their past lives more vividly. A bodhisattva can recall past lives over a span of several tens of thousands of years, whereas a tathagata can recall much further into the past. If tathagatas put their minds to it, they can recall things that happened hundreds of thousands or even a million years ago. When it comes to the grand tathagatas of the ninth dimension, they can recall memories from the time of Creation. They can recall every event—how they came into existence hundreds of millions of years ago, how the Earth was created, and how humankind has been evolving.

So, although spirits can recall the memories of their past lives, how far back and to what scale they can recall depends on their position in the Spirit World. It is like climbing an observation tower. The higher you go, the farther you can see, but a lower tower will only allow you to see the nearby area, and you will not be able to see anything if you go down into the basement. The same is true with the other world; in the basement, that is to say, in hell, you cannot see anything, but the higher up you go, the farther you can see, which means you can recall memories from ancient times.

In summary, how far back spirits can recall the memories of their past lives differs from spirit to spirit. Some can only recall their immediate past life, whereas others can recall several lives back, yet others can recall several dozen or even hundreds of lives in the past. This is very mystical yet true. The more you cultivate your spiritual awareness, the more you can see the past, the present, and the future in the truest sense.

10

The Road to Evolution

In this chapter, I talked about many things regarding the fourth dimension, that is to say, about the life that starts when a spirit leaves this third dimensional earthly world and returns to the other world. But many people probably wonder why that is how things go. Why do heaven and hell exist? Why aren't we taught about them while we are alive in this world? Why do the physical body and the spirit exist? Why can't we live as spirits both in this world and in the other world? Many people may be questioning these things.

The transition from a physical body to a spirit is like a cicada shedding its skin and flying off into the sky. After many years of living underground, cicada nymphs emerge to climb up a tree, shed their skin on the trunk, and spread their wings until they eventually fly up into the open sky. This illustrates our transition well.

We can also see this in an ugly green caterpillar crawling on leaves that turns into a chrysalis before we know it and eventually into a beautiful cabbage butterfly or swallowtail butterfly. As a matter of fact, it is Buddha who created this process—caterpillars turning into chrysalises, then into butterflies. He created them to teach humans about the process of reincarnation. This is how humans evolve as they change their form of existence.

You may wonder why a caterpillar turns into a butterfly, but that is how Buddha created them to be and no one can deny this fact. Creatures with dozens of stubby legs wiggling on leaves and munching them with ugly expressions on their face eventually grow wings and fly up into the vast sky—this process hints at the spiritual evolution of human beings.

Why did Buddha create such a process? Simply put, here, you can see Buddha's Mercy at work. He could have created butterflies so that they could fly from the time they were born, but by experiencing a restricted life beforehand where they can only crawl on the ground, they get to feel how wonderful it is to be able to fly. By showing humans the process of caterpillars turning into butterflies, Buddha is teaching them the meaning of life. No human would wish to become a cabbage butterfly, but how wonderful must it be to fly freely in the vast sky; humans can never experience something like that. Butterflies probably know a kind of happiness that humans can never experience. Here lies Buddha's Mercy. Buddha has given such happiness to butterflies.

In the same way, humans live a restricted life as they dwell in a physical body, but they eventually cast off their bodies and return to their true form as spirits. At that time, they will feel several times or dozens of times stronger, what great beings humans are. While on earth, humans come to feel impatient, exhausted, or helpless because they cannot easily achieve everything they want, but in the other world, their thoughts manifest themselves instantly. Upon discovering this ability, they think, "This never happened on earth. It is tens of times more wonderful than what I experienced on earth!"

Buddha prepared such a wonderful road to spiritual evolution for humans; this is how the other world and this world work. This mechanism exists because, without shedding our old skin or without sublimating to the next stage, we cannot feel true happiness.

You are a spiritual being, which means you have the same nature as Buddha. Everyone will be able to experience and appreciate for themselves that they have the same nature as Buddha. This is an amazing experience. You are living in such a wonderful world.

Even if you suffer in hell for some 100 or 200 years, in the long term, this experience will serve as a whetstone to polish your soul and guide you to further evolution. In other words, you will be placed in an environment that urges you to reflect squarely on the shortcomings you must work on the most. So hell is not a completely bad experience; the spirits of hell are also in the process of evolution.

However, this is not to say that hell should be left as it is. Spirits are indeed suffering while in hell. To help them get out of their suffering, we need to guide them so that they can realize where they have gone wrong as soon as possible so they can start walking in the right direction. This is the right approach and the right method that accords with Buddha's Will. Although heavenly spirits are making an effort to do this, the spirits in hell also need to realize their mistakes on their own. That is why hell exists. Even if they may seem to have regressed a little, in the long run, each spirit is walking on the road to evolution. There is no doubt that this is true.

CHAPTER TWO

The World of
the Fifth Dimension

1

Into the World of Goodness

In Chapter One, I talked about various secrets of the world that humans first enter after casting off their physical bodies and leaving the earthly world as spirits. Now, in this chapter, I will talk about a dimension of a higher level.

In modern physics, it is becoming clear that the world we live in is part of a multi-layered structure consisting of the third, fourth, fifth, sixth, seventh, eighth, and ninth dimensions. Each dimension encompasses the one below it to create a vast, onion-like structure with the third dimension being enveloped by the fourth, the fourth by the fifth, the fifth by the sixth, and so on. Science presents this kind of worldview.

If you explore the other world firsthand, you will find that this is entirely true. The spirits of the fourth dimension are not living in a world that is completely different from the third dimension. The fourth dimension co-exists with the third dimension and exerts various influences over it. Then, the fifth dimension exists above the fourth dimension.

One thing that is interesting about this structure is that, while the inhabitants of the higher dimensions can influence those in the lower dimensions, the inhabitants of the lower dimensions cannot influence those in the higher dimensions.

There is such a law. The spirits of the fifth dimension can freely go to the fourth dimension and offer various kinds of guidance to the spirits there. But there is a principle that the spirits living in the fourth dimension cannot visit the fifth dimension. There are some exceptions, but this is the general rule.

Theoretically, this may not be easy to understand, but in reality, this is how it is in the other world. Buddhism also teaches that there are different spiritual levels or hierarchies in the other world, and so do mysticism and theosophy. It is mentioned in ancient documents as well. They all teach that the world is not just divided into two—this world and the other world—but the other world is divided into many different realms, not only horizontally but also vertically in terms of space.

In 18th-century Europe, there was a psychic named Emanuel Swedenborg. He explored the other world, or the Spirit World, and left behind a written record of what he experienced. In his book, he said something along the lines of, "When I looked up, I felt that there was an invisible, transparent screen-like layer covering the sky, and there seemed to be yet another world beyond it." In reality, this is not something that can be explained visually, but there are indeed different spiritual levels.

So, what is the difference between the inhabitants of the fourth dimension and those of the fifth dimension?

The fourth dimension is the first step into the spiritual world and the inhabitants there are like first-graders in elementary school. They do not yet fully understand the relationship between the spiritual body and the physical body or between the soul and material things. They still live in a way that is a mixture of earthly and spiritual lifestyles.

As they continue to live in the fourth dimension, their souls gradually evolve; some will only take a few days or years, whereas others will take as long as a couple of decades or a few hundred years. When their souls evolve, they will be guided by angels or their guardian and guiding spirits and ascend to the dimension above—the fifth dimension.

What kind of world is the fifth dimension? Put simply, it is a world of "goodness." The fifth dimension is a world of good. Souls that gather there are inclined toward goodness or what is good instead of what is evil. They all share this tendency. When facing good and evil, souls of the fifth dimension have abandoned evil and chosen good. What is more, they are vaguely aware that Buddha or God expects humans to be good. This is the fifth dimension.

2

A Spiritual Awakening

"Goodness"—the characteristic of souls in the fifth dimension—is not merely goodness in contrast to evil; it means awakening to our true nature as a child of Buddha. To put it simply, it is a spiritual awakening.

Spiritual and material things co-exist in life on earth. Humans are surrounded by material things in their lives on earth, and they constantly think about how to make a living, earn a salary, or buy, use, and discard material objects. But despite being surrounded by material things, some people engage in activities, for example, in the evening or during the weekend, that will bring them spiritual joy. They are recognized as wonderful people. Of course, other people never experience spiritual joy and instead lose themselves in gambling and other worldly pleasures. But most people do not find their souls satisfied by this and seem to feel nostalgia for something spiritual that can be gained through reading, music, or art. They do these activities out of nostalgia for the world they originally came from.

The fifth dimension is called the "Goodness Realm" or the "Spiritual Realm" because the people who gather there have awakened to spirituality. The inhabitants of the Goodness Realm are clearly aware that they are spiritual beings.

On the other hand, the fourth dimension is called the "Astral Realm." Some of the inhabitants there are not yet fully aware that they are spirits, whereas others are more or less aware of it. Their level of awareness varies, but in any case, they have yet to fully grasp the true nature of spirituality or fully recognize themselves as spirits. They are yet to reach the awareness where they strive to seek the goodness that is within the true nature of the spirit.

Those in the fifth dimension know that the true nature of a human being is a spirit, and are proactively seeking something good. What is more, everyone has faith in Buddha or God, although they may not be aware of it. Who they believe in depends on their religious background, but the spirits of the fifth dimensional Goodness Realm all have some kind of a good, religious heart. Every day, they feel the presence of Buddha or God close by and live for His sake. The types of work that people have on earth still exist in the fifth dimension and some spirits are actually engaging in such work. For example, some are working as carpenters and some are selling goods to others. Their work is to provide what others need. Besides those types of work, some spirits are working to make life more convenient for others, much like the service industries on earth.

In this way, many spirits of the fifth dimensional Goodness Realm still hold occupations that are found on earth, but this is not because they need money. It is because they find joy when the work they do pleases Buddha or God.

3

The Joy of the Soul

The spirits of the fourth dimension cannot yet fully appreciate the joy of the soul. What they experience is "amazement of the soul"; they are amazed that they are actually souls and find their experiences new and exciting. They are learning that spirits can do all kinds of mysterious things. On the other hand, the inhabitants of the fifth dimensional Goodness Realm can feel the joy of the soul.

This means that those in the fourth dimensional Astral Realm cannot yet fully distinguish life in the fourth dimension from life on earth. They are still "wearing" an astral body which is like a kind of physical body or clothes. But spirits cast away this astral body before going to the fifth dimensional Goodness Realm, so the vibrations of their souls become more refined. In other words, spirits in the fifth dimension live purely as souls. The soul refers to a spirit with the awareness of a human, and it begins to feel joy.

What kind of joy is it? What kind of joy do souls feel? In general, there are two occasions when souls feel joy.

The first is when they feel they are improving. Souls feel joy when they feel they have improved. When do they feel they have improved? It is when they can confirm that they are good beings. And when can they confirm this? It is when they feel that they are able to help others. This is when souls feel joy.

The same is true of humans living on earth. When someone says to you, "I'm glad you are here," or "Things went well thanks to you," you naturally feel very happy. That is because recognizing that you are a helpful being to others brings you the joy of self-expansion and self-improvement. When you feel that other people are glad that you exist and that you are not just living for your own sake, it means the life you are living is worth more than just one person's life. In other words, self-expansion or self-improvement means you are living in a way that is worth several times more than just living for your own sake. So, the first occasion when souls feel joy is when they find themselves to be helpful to others and confirm to themselves that they are good beings.

What, then, is the second occasion when souls feel joy? It is when they acquire new knowledge. The first is when they make others happy or are being helpful to others and the second is when they gain new knowledge.

The knowledge I am talking about here is not the kind that you can gain by studying for an exam in a worldly sense, but spiritual discoveries regarding the world created by Buddha. Souls feel joy when they make such discoveries.

The soul has various characteristics, abilities, and powers, but souls of the fifth dimensional Goodness Realm are not yet aware of them all.

Some souls still eat food in the fifth dimension. Although they know very well that they do not have to eat to survive, some of them find joy in eating whereas others find joy in making food. Those who used to be farmers while on earth and truly enjoy growing crops are still working in farms in the other world, doing things like planting rice. These kinds of souls reside in the fifth dimension.

However, they gradually realize that this is not a true way of life and understand that humans can feel spiritual joy without having to cultivate crops. For example, they realize that the sweet potatoes they made were not of third dimensional material but were made spiritually in their minds. And they learn that the richer and more affluent their minds become, the more beautiful the sweet potatoes they can harvest. There are various scientific methods for watering and fertilizing crops on earth, but this is not necessarily the case in the other world. You can harvest beautiful, fresh sweet potatoes by caring for them and putting your heart into cultivating them.

In this way, the spirits of the fifth dimension learn how things work in the spiritual world. They gradually come to know the true nature of the world where thoughts become reality. This experience of "knowing" brings them the second form of joy.

4

The Light Flows

I described that souls feel joy on two occasions: one is when they are being helpful to others and the other is when they acquire new spiritual knowledge. Now, let me talk more about acquiring spiritual knowledge.

The souls of the fourth dimensional Astral Realm are not yet fully aware that the true nature of a human, or the true nature of a spirit, is light that has split off from Buddha. But in the fifth dimensional Goodness Realm, souls gradually awaken to the true nature of light. They become capable of distinguishing between different intensities of light. They also realize that the real energy which is the "light of Buddha," as opposed to the light of a fluorescent lamp or candle, is flowing in their dimension. This is an unfamiliar, yet indescribable sensation.

Eventually, the spirits of the fifth dimensional Goodness Realm come to know where this light comes from. There is a large sun in the sky that is different from the one we see in the third dimension; it is called the Spiritual Sun. What is the true nature of the Spiritual Sun? It is, in fact, the spiritual entity of the sun that shines on Earth in the third dimension. In the same way that a soul dwells in the physical body of a human being and a great soul called Earth Consciousness dwells in the huge spherical physical body of Earth, there is also a great soul, a great spiritual body, that dwells in the sun. This means that in the sun that emits physical light dwells a spiritual sun that emits spiritual light. The Spiritual Sun in the other world is the spiritual body of the sun that sheds brilliant light onto the earth. The Spiritual Sun sheds light onto the other world.

So, the sun not only supplies this world with energy such as heat, but it also provides beings in the other world with real spiritual energy. The Earth, a member of the solar system, also exists thanks to the energy that comes from the grand consciousness that governs the solar system.

The energy body that dwells in the sun is the stellar consciousness of our solar system. It is an eleventh dimensional being called Solar System Consciousness. This consciousness sheds the light of seven colors onto the Earth through the tenth dimensional planetary consciousnesses of Earth. There are only three of them: Grand Sun Consciousness, Moon Consciousness, and Earth Consciousness. This light or energy is then split into different kinds of light through the ten spirits of the ninth dimension and flows into the earthly world as well as into all the realms of the other world.

The spirits of the fifth dimensional Goodness Realm do not know all these facts yet, but they know that the Spiritual Sun provides them with energy and power, much like the sun on earth. They learn that their lives are sustained by receiving light energy from the Spiritual Sun and that they are able to live because of this energy. So, those living in the fifth dimension never forget their gratitude toward the Spiritual Sun. First and foremost, they are deeply grateful to the Spiritual Sun, which comes before they develop simple faith in Buddha or God. They frequently worship the Spiritual Sun with their hands together in prayer in the morning and evening. In this way, the fifth dimensional world is a place where you can feel how light flows.

5

The Feeling of Love

Another distinct characteristic of the spirits in the fifth dimension is that they awaken to the feeling called love. In the earthly world, there is love between a man and a woman, between a parent and a child, between friends, or between a master and a disciple. Compared to these, love becomes purer in the fifth dimensional Goodness Realm.

The feeling of love is quite difficult to express on earth, but in the other world, it feels very real. When you love someone, your vibration of love is transmitted directly to him or her. So the spirit receiving it will very strongly feel that they are loved, and it will bring joy to their soul.

In this world, the feeling of love cannot be felt so clearly. Because of this, people often become lovesick; they are not sure whether they are loved or not. They walk an emotional tightrope when it comes to relationship issues. Because they are unsure whether or not they are loved, even if the other person loves them, they become suspicious and think that he or she is just treating them exactly the same way they treat others, or they become resentful thinking that he or she does not really love them.

In the fifth dimensional Goodness Realm, however, people have the ability to tell whether they are being loved or not as if they have an indicator or barometer because they can directly feel how other spirits feel. This feeling is similar to how you can sense the difference in light intensity between a fluorescent light and an incandescent light bulb, or between 60-watt, 100-watt, and 200-watt light bulbs. It means that a spirit's emotions will be conveyed with certainty, including the strength of their love for another.

In this way, the Goodness Realm of the fifth dimension is a place where what you think and feel is transmitted directly to other people without having to speak; others will immediately know what you have thought in your mind. This is the very reason why the spirits of hell cannot stay in the fifth dimension. The spirits of hell are filled with hatred, envy, complaints, anger, and insatiable desires, and these emotions will be transmitted to others. If there was even one spirit with such emotions living in the fifth dimension, it would no longer be heaven.

The inhabitants of the fifth dimensional Goodness Realm all have feelings of love. Their love may vary in its amount or level—it could be great or small, or high or low—but love is common in everyone. Each spirit is like a power source that radiates a current of love.

Once they understand love as a real feeling, they sometimes receive lectures about love from higher beings of the sixth dimension. They will be told, "When you are loved by someone, you feel love flowing into you like an electric current, don't you? You feel the warmth in your heart and become happy, right? That is the love of Buddha."

Although the spirits of the fifth dimension still cannot clearly understand Buddha, they can feel what Buddha is like. When high spirits describe Buddha to the spirits in the fifth dimension, they often talk like this:

"You can probably feel love. The greatest form of love is the Sun which sits in the sky of the Spirit World. It provides us with heat and energy without receiving anything in return; it supplies us with the energy of life without asking for a single penny. This unconditional love, or mercy, is the true nature of Buddha. When you love each other, you feel the vibration of love fill up your heart and you become very happy, don't you? This proves that you are children of Buddha and that you are essentially part of Buddha's energy."

The high spirits patiently teach in this way. This is the primary education about love. At this stage, the spirits in the fifth dimension are yet to reach a level where they can practice giving love like the spirits in the Bodhisattva Realm do, but they learn the basics of love, such as what love is, what it is like to be loved, and what it means to give love. They gradually learn that it is better to be loved than not and that to love others is a wonderful thing. Eventually, they come to understand that love is not love if they have a desire to protect themselves or to benefit themselves only.

6

Sadness and Suffering

From ancient times, it has been believed that heaven is an eternal paradise where sadness and suffering do not exist. But do sadness and suffering really disappear, or cease to exist, when you return to the fourth dimension (other than hell) or the fifth dimension? Let me expound on this topic.

It is generally believed that sadness and suffering are specific to hell and that these feelings do not exist in heaven. But does this mean that Buddha did not originally expect humans to cry and shed tears? Are the spirits in heaven only allowed to laugh? Let us think about these points.

Human beings experience basic emotions of joy, anger, sadness, and pleasure and it is an undeniable fact that these feelings exist. The opposite of joy is sadness, for example, but we cannot simply say that sadness is the absence of joy.

Since long ago, there have been debates between the philosophy of monism and the philosophy of dualism. Monists often say, "Evil is the absence of good" or "There is no such thing as coldness. Coldness is merely the absence of heat or warmth." Ralph Waldo Emerson, an American philosopher who was a proponent of positive thinking and one of the leaders of the New Thought movement, also advocated this kind of philosophy.

This philosophy is true if you focus on one side of things; you feel cold when there is no heat, and there is no goodness where evil prevails. However, this does not explain everything. We cry when we feel sad, but this does not necessarily mean that we cry because we do not feel joy. We do not shed tears just because we feel no joy. So, you must know that sadness is an emotion that actually exists.

Then, what about suffering as opposed to pleasure? Is it true that only pleasure exists and there is no such thing as suffering? Is suffering just the absence of pleasure? Let us think about these questions.

Suffering, in fact, also exists. For example, if you play tennis or some other sport for an hour or two, you will sweat but feel refreshed afterward. For you to feel refreshed, you needed to sweat first. In other words, the physical fatigue and pain that you felt were what led you to feel refreshed.

So, I must say that this world and the other world have a dualistic aspect for the most part. The Ultimate Buddha is absolute light, absolute goodness, and absolute love; He only consists of good elements. But He created this third dimensional world on earth and the lower spiritual worlds of the fourth and fifth dimensions to allow souls to make progress and improve themselves. This was the main purpose of creating these worlds.

In these worlds souls can compare themselves relative to each other, which makes them more likely to make progress and improve themselves; without competing against each other and going through suffering to polish their souls, it would be difficult for them to improve. Although a monistic world where only pleasure exists may seem attractive, in a sense, it is like living a lukewarm life. That is why Buddha gives what feels like sadness or suffering to people in the earthly world and lower spiritual realms as an expedient way to improve themselves.

To give you an example, even the spirits residing in the fifth dimensional Goodness Realm sometimes struggle to achieve self-realization. Spirits in the fifth dimension pray too just like people on earth, but there are times when their wishes are fully heard and times when they are not. They cannot really tell whether their prayers are righteous or not, but from the perspective of the spirits of higher dimensions, their prayers are sometimes judged as premature and something that should not be granted yet. When their prayers are not granted, in other words, when their wishes are not fulfilled, they feel sad or pain to some extent. This means that fifth dimensional spirits, too, are undergoing basic spiritual training to strengthen their souls.

7

Nourishment for the Soul

There is a school of thought that says, "Sadness and suffering are mere illusions, and they, in essence, do not exist. Sadness and suffering are not real entities. They are simply expressions of a deluded mind and are not real." But I do not agree with this idea.

The Primordial Buddha, by His very nature, cannot make progress or undergo development. As the Primordial Buddha, He is perfect and flawless and embodies supreme goodness, supreme love, and supreme happiness. In other words, He is the ultimate good, the ultimate truth, and the ultimate beauty. Because He has this nature, the Primordial Buddha cannot experience progress or development, or the joy that comes with it.

To experience these things, the Primordial Buddha created this Great Universe. He enjoyed creating it as if making a garden. He placed rocks, dug ponds and released fish into them, planted trees of different sizes, grew fruit, and sometimes planted weeds. He made every effort to add more variety to His garden. The Primordial Buddha even created things that appear imperfect to human eyes to give contrast to His garden. It is all right for a few weeds to grow. There are tall trees as well as short trees. There is raised land like small hills, but also sunken land like ponds. The garden of the Primordial Buddha is made up of a variety of things, and He is enjoying His gardening. In the same way, the Primordial Buddha allows things that are not real entities, such as sadness and suffering, to exist under strict conditions and for specific purposes. This is the truth.

As I said earlier, we cannot necessarily say that the absence of joy causes sadness; we do not shed tears just because there is no joy. When we cry, there is also a feeling of sadness at work. In the same way, we do not suffer as soon as we do not feel pleasure; there is usually something that causes our suffering.

Sadness and suffering do exist, but it is not because they are good things in and of themselves. The truth is that sadness and suffering exist in this world, as well as in the fourth and fifth dimensions, for souls to make a great leap in their advancement. People experience sadness and pain when things do not easily turn out the way they want. When they face an outcome that is far from what they wanted, they may suffer or feel sadness and sometimes even shed bitter tears. However, there is a greater meaning to why people shed tears; through tears of struggle, they develop themselves to a higher level. Similarly, when people sweat from doing hard work, it enables them to feel accomplished and refreshed afterward.

So, we must not look at this world as a world of suffering or a world of sadness. Rather, we need to know that, although suffering and sadness exist, they are there to act as a whetstone to polish our souls. There is a Japanese saying *"gyoku-seki konko"* which is used to say there is a mix of good and bad things. Visually, the phrase can be explained as a bag full of gems and stones. The gems will brush against the stones and the gems will get smoother and more polished as a result.

Although humans are meant to experience sadness and suffering, these things are not supposed to last forever. They are only allowed to exist temporarily as nourishment for the soul. Ultimately, souls are expected to grow and develop toward a world of joy and pleasure, a world of everlasting happiness, and a world of everlasting paradise. So, please remember that the best way to understand pain and suffering is that they are only allowed to exist as nourishment for the soul.

8

To Ones Closer to the Light

I have spoken about how sadness and suffering exist as nourishment for the soul. You may wonder what comes after you go through these struggles.

Have you ever heard of the phrase, "Light shines forth when you break through the depths of despair"? Some people have said, "When I hit rock bottom, a ray of light shined forth from the depths of my despair. I thought that light only shines from above, but when I broke through the depths of my misery, light shined forth from below."

The playwright and artist, William Shakespeare, wrote various tragedies because he wanted to show people the light that is found at the depths of tragedy. His message to the world was: when you break through the depths of tragedy, you will find the truth of human nature, and at the core of this nature lies an inner light. This means that comedy and happy stories are not the only things that encourage people to make progress. You may get closer to the light sooner through events that appear to be tragic in this world.

Many people in the world begrudge their fate and say, "Why am I the only one to be born under an unlucky star? Why do I have to suffer so much?" It may be that they lost their parents in their childhood, they could not go to school due to financial difficulties, they could not get married, or they could get married but lost their partner. Or, perhaps they went through a divorce, were not blessed with children, had children but lost them while they were still young, or had children that became delinquent. If you count miseries like this one by one, you could go on forever because there are an infinite number of seeds of sadness in this world.

But are these sad experiences or misfortunes totally meaningless? Do they do us any good? Before being born into this world, humans lived in heaven where there was not much sadness or suffering. Spirits may sometimes experience their prayers and wishes going unanswered, but there is nothing that tries to intentionally harm them. On the other hand, in this world, people may be harmed or struck by misfortune as though they are at the mercy of fate.

In the Old Testament, there is the story of Job. All kinds of misfortune befall Job until he finally curses God. But God tells him, "Job, are you so wise that you can judge the Will of God? Be humble. Do you really understand My intentions?" God says this to Job but what He truly means is, "God uses various 'stage settings' to help humans evolve further." You can interpret his story in this way.

Therefore, you must not think about things solely from a worldly perspective. For example, you should know that the deceased person who left you could now be leading a wonderful life in the other world. After all, those who are given many ordeals are that much closer to the light. Heaven can be near you in times of joy, but heaven is also close in times of despair. When you break through the depths of sadness and experience the light, heaven will appear. People in this world need to know this.

9

About Nobility

Next, I would like to talk about the nobility of the soul. Having a noble soul means to have a noble character or an exalted character. Both noble and exalted mean "outstanding" or "excellent." In other words, nobility means having an outstanding character, which is extremely valuable. When do we consider that someone has a noble soul or a noble mind?

Imagine a person who is the firstborn son of a very rich family and lives in a large mansion with a private swimming pool. As the first son, he is attended to by servants and lives just the way he wants to. He is smart by nature, good-looking, and loved by many women. Even after going out into the working world, he is loved by many, treated well, and given a high position. He leads a good life and, eventually, his life will come to an end. Do you feel that someone who led a life like that has a noble soul? Would you see someone who lived in such a fortunate environment as a great figure?

I believe that one of the reasons great figures are regarded as great by the world is that they have overcome some kind of difficulties or hardships. That is what makes them great figures. For instance, there was Dr. Albert Schweitzer, a high spirit who carried out missionary work in the harsh

African environment. There was Thomas Edison, who became the world's most famous inventor despite having quit elementary school and receiving no further school education. There was Abraham Lincoln, who was born into a poor family but studied hard under tough circumstances and went on to become the president of the United States through strenuous effort. There was also Mahatma Gandhi, the father of Indian independence. He, too, was a high spirit; he bore responsibility for his country and rose to confront the mighty British Empire. When we look at the lives of these people, we can see the real meaning of sufferings and difficulties. We realize that sufferings and difficulties are not mere obstacles but a means to make the path or footsteps of people's lives more beautiful.

Of course, this is not only true for people of modern times but also for those who lived in the past. For example, Shakyamuni Buddha of India was born into a royal family and lived in comfort, but he made a crucial decision at the age of 29 to leave the royal palace and set out on the road to enlightenment.

When we strive to achieve a higher purpose regardless of any hardships that come our way, the nobility of our souls shines forth. I believe this nobility is a light that illuminates even people of later generations. I find great comfort in the fact that there are many great figures shining like bright stars throughout the history of humankind.

In the course of our lives, all kinds of sufferings and difficulties may befall us; they can happen to me and to each person who is reading this book. In reality, there is no end to the number of people in the past who were confronted with sufferings and difficulties. Those who were overwhelmed by them have sunk into oblivion whereas those who were able to overcome them have been rewarded with the nobility of the soul. If the life of Jesus had consisted of nothing but sufferings and difficulties without him overcoming them, he would not have gone down in history as a great figure. But because he displayed the nobility of his soul through his ordeals, he became a Great Light that has guided people of later generations.

10

The Time to Be Guided

If you are currently blessed with a wonderful environment, you should be grateful for it and think that it is your duty to make efforts to improve yourself even further. The better the environment you find yourself in, or the more talented or gifted you are compared to others, the harder you must work on yourself relative to others.

On the other hand, if you are obviously at a disadvantage in terms of your circumstances, upbringing, talent, or financial situation, or if you are born with an illness or are suffering from a physical disability, you must not keep complaining about it. As I said, these difficulties have manifested themselves as a means to help you evolve and develop further.

If you complain about your difficulties or begrudge them, what good will that do for your soul? Will it help you develop your soul? You may have to bear a "cross" on your back, but only when you strive to live your life with it and bear its weight will your difficulties become nourishment for your soul. I believe that it is precisely by leading your life in this way that you will be able to emit light from within.

Of course, there is no need for you to ask for sufferings or hardships to befall you. You do not need to pray to

God by saying, "O God, please grant me more sufferings and hardships." However, you can strive to develop strong willpower that enables you to overcome any sufferings or hardships. Instead of just bemoaning what you lack, you must have a strong will to find the true value of what you have been given and courageously stand up with it as your weapon.

Some people are blind but can speak eloquently; some people cannot walk but are skillful with their hands; some people are not smart but have healthy bodies; some people are ill but have sharp minds. So, before comparing yourself to others and bemoaning or cursing what you lack, you should consider what you have been given and strive to develop your strengths to the best of your ability. In doing so, you will find clues to solve your "workbook of life."

Each person's life is full of mysteries; it is a workbook of problems to be solved. But there are always clues to help you solve your workbook. When you look at yourself from another person's point of view, you will most definitely find something you excel at compared to others. Of course, there must also be something you are extremely poor at compared to others. When you compare your personality, talents, or physical features to those of others, you will find that you either excel or lack in a particular area. That area is precisely where the clues can be found to solve your workbook of life.

It is important to ask yourself, "Why have I been given this challenge?" and actively strive to find the answer. The challenge you face clearly shows one of the purposes of your soul training in this lifetime. You may have various disadvantages such as physical, mental, or intellectual disabilities, but they reveal your purpose and mission in this lifetime.

The moment you come to realize this is a moment when you are being guided. When you become aware of your fate and are determined to face it bravely, courage and power will well up from within you. At that time, the high spirits in the other world or your guardian and guiding spirits will aid you with great power. So, first recognize the clues that are hidden in your workbook of life. As you try to solve your problems using those clues, you will surely receive great power from high spirits.

Once humans have learned the true nature of the soul, they often realize that humans are existences that must make efforts for all of eternity. That is right. Because humans are living an eternal life, they must strive to overcome various challenges that are given to them, and only through those experiences can humans gain nobility, light, and nourishment of the soul. Recognize your problems and find the clues to solve them. Cherish these moments—they are times when you are being guided.

CHAPTER THREE

The World of
the Sixth Dimension

1

The Main Road of Evolution

In this chapter, I will mainly talk about the aspects of the sixth dimensional Light Realm. The last two chapters were about the fourth and fifth dimensions, the realms that average people return to shortly after death. But from the sixth dimension, we step into a world known as the world of high spirits. The reason the sixth dimension is referred to in this way is that, since ancient times, it has been said that the spirits who are regarded as "gods" reside there. So who are these gods? Let me start by briefly explaining this.

Obviously, the gods who reside in the sixth dimensional Light Realm are not the Creator or the God of Creation. There is no such "God" in this dimension. The spirits who are regarded as gods in the sixth dimension are those who were virtuous and made great achievements, or demonstrated tremendous power, while they were living as human beings on earth. They were admired by the people of the world, who thought things like, "They are extraordinary. I can't believe they are the same human beings like us. They must be god-like people." One example of such an extraordinary person was the Japanese politician Sugawara no Michizane [845 – 903 AD], who is now enshrined as the god of learning. People, like him, who were enshrined as a god soon after death, and whose minds were not inclined to hell, return to the sixth dimensional Light Realm (although some people are unreasonably enshrined based on the mistaken views of people on earth).

To put it simply, the spirits who can be in the sixth dimensional Light Realm are those who earn the respect of others. What kind of people are respected by others? They are virtuous people who are capable of leaving behind incredible achievements that are far beyond human capabilities. In other words, they are more evolved than others. For that reason, people have sometimes been in awe of their spiritual powers and abilities and revered them as gods. Many Japanese gods of ancient times are among those living in the sixth dimension.

2

Knowing God

I said that many spirits who are regarded as gods reside in the sixth dimensional Light Realm, but I must explain further what God is. This has long been an important theme in the fields of philosophy, religion, and theology. Some have declared, "To know God is to know everything," while others have asserted, "Humans were not created in God's image; it is humans who created God in their own image. God is merely a figment of their imagination." No one has been able to offer clear answers to the question, "What is God?"

So let me share with you my current ideas about what "God" is. First, we need to distinguish God (or Buddha), who is the Creator of the world, from "gods" who are not the Creator.

Christianity often refers to "the Father, the Son, and the Holy Spirit." When they refer to God, they sometimes mean "the Holy Spirit," and at other times, "the Son," which means Jesus Christ, and at times, only "the Father." In general, we can say that a god, in the broad meaning, is a spiritual being who is superior to ordinary human beings. So in that sense, the Holy Spirit can also be referred to as god. In fact, the gods living in the sixth dimensional Light Realm are the ones referred to as "the Holy Spirit" in Christianity. However, God the Creator is a Being that exists in a dimension of a much, much higher level.

Then, are all the spirits of the sixth dimension gods? No, they are not. There are different levels even within the sixth dimension. People living on earth may find it difficult to understand what this means. They usually imagine that transparent layers in the air divide the sixth dimension into different levels, but that is not the case. It is not like a high-rise apartment building where people live on different floors. To understand this, we need to remember that spirits no longer have physical bodies. Rather, they are living as consciousness.

Consciousness is a kind of energy body similar to electromagnetic waves, electrical energy, or gaseous bodies. It is a body of life energy with a unique, distinctive character— this is the true nature of a spirit. I have told you that the sixth dimension has different levels, but they are actually the differences in the wavelengths of these life energies. So different levels do not mean upper or lower in a physical sense but are the differences between higher spiritual wavelengths and lower spiritual wavelengths.

Suppose you stir up a glass of muddy water and leave it for a while. The heavier particles will eventually move from the top to the bottom. The water will become clearer higher up in the glass and darker lower down. In the same way, the more coarse a spirit's wavelength, the lower the spirit sinks in the Spirit World. That is, if a spiritual body carries earthly, material weight, its consciousness becomes heavy and it sinks lower down. On the other hand, a god-like, refined consciousness that has little attachment to earthly matters will rise higher. So spirits, which can be considered as consciousnesses with certain wavelengths or energy bodies, exist in different places according to their wavelengths. This is how you should understand it.

3

Different Stages of Enlightenment

The other world is a world of consciousnesses, and there are different levels to these consciousnesses. Knowing this truth is the first step to enlightenment.

The word "enlightenment" has many meanings. The basic level of enlightenment is to understand that a human being is not just a physical existence. Understanding this truth alone is already a form of enlightenment. Not many spirits in the fourth dimensional Astral Realm have clearly awakened to the fact that a human being is not a physical existence. Most are still unsure of what they really are; they live their lives as if they still have a physical body, but at the same time, as if they do not.

There is also the enlightenment that is attained when a spirit ascends to heaven from hell. In this case, enlightenment means to attain the most basic understanding of the truth that human beings should not live solely based on a desire to protect themselves and that they must live for the benefit of others. Spirits in hell follow their selfish desires; they are self-centered and only think about themselves. They only want what is best for them and care less about others. These are the types of spirits that reside in hell. They all say, "What's wrong with living for myself?"

However, after decades or centuries of living in hell surrounded by like-minded spirits with self-protective and selfish desires, they eventually grow sick of these desires and change their ways of thinking. The time comes when they long for a world of comfort and peace. This is the first level of enlightenment that spirits need to attain to ascend from hell to heaven. When this happens, they return to the Fairy Realm in the upper part of the fourth dimension, and then to the Goodness Realm of the fifth dimension, as I explained earlier.

The fifth dimension is known as the "Goodness Realm" or the "Spiritual Realm." Those who reside there have awakened to their spirituality—they are spiritually awakened souls—or have awakened to the importance of goodness. But, although they are good-hearted souls, they are not very serious about seeking enlightenment. They are not conscious enough of Buddha or God.

In contrast to this, there are no so-called atheists in the sixth dimensional Light Realm. To a greater or lesser extent, the spirits there understand that a Great Being allows humans and spirits to live. The only difference is what they refer to this Being as—Buddha or God. It differs depending on the individual. Their approaches to seeking this Great Being also differ. Many professional priests can be found in the sixth dimension, including Buddhist monks, Shinto ministers, and

Christian priests. They earnestly explore and organize their thoughts about Buddha or God.

There are also other kinds of souls. They are people who made progress in their professions while they were alive in the earthly world. Although they did not necessarily seek Buddha or God, they evolved considerably through their professions. These souls also live in the sixth dimension.

There are indeed a great number of scholars in the sixth dimension. Many university professors and other excellent teachers whose minds were not inclined to hell have returned there. In addition to university professors, there are also many people with respectable professions such as doctors, lawyers, judges, and so on. Pure-hearted politicians and bureaucrats have also returned to the sixth dimensional Light Realm. If we look at them, we can see that no matter what their profession is, they are all highly evolved souls. Those who have highly advanced as spirits by developing their artistic talents, such as painters and musicians, also reside in the sixth dimensional Light Realm.

What is the main work of the spirits of the sixth dimension? Buddhist monks, Shinto ministers, and Christian priests guide people working in religion on earth. Those who used to be politicians in their lives guide the politicians on earth, whereas former bureaucrats guide the people working in government offices. Those who were artists send inspiration to artists on earth, whereas those who were university professors give inspiration to scholars and students studying on earth. In doing so, the guiding spirits themselves, too, continue to pursue enlightenment in their own specialized field. By teaching what they have grasped to those who are still progressing, they accumulate experiences in preparation for engaging in the work of a bodhisattva. In other words, they experience the work of serving others.

In summary, the common value of the sixth dimensional Light Realm is usefulness—being of service to others. To be of use to the world, bring progress to the world, or contribute to the development of the world—these are the main principles that the spirits of the sixth dimension live by. Although their work is still not enough to be called "love" in the truest sense and is at the stage before that, it will surely sprout into love in due time.

4

An Ocean of Light

Now, let me describe the sixth dimensional Light Realm in a more visual way. As I have written in various books, the higher the dimension you go up to in the other world, the brighter the light becomes. Indeed, the amount of light increases tremendously as you enter the sixth dimensional Light Realm.

Sometimes, when you are walking or driving through mountains, you may suddenly come to an open view. Far below, you can see a town at the foot of the mountain or a vast ocean in the distance. You may have experienced a moment when great scenery has suddenly opened up before you. Spirits who enter the sixth dimensional Light Realm go through a similar experience.

In a way, it is like an ocean of light. When you first enter the sixth dimensional Light Realm, you will find it too bright; it feels as if you are gazing at a bright sea in summer that is reflecting sunlight. It takes some time before your eyes get used to it. I am not saying this just as a metaphor; there is indeed an extremely beautiful ocean in the sixth dimensional Light Realm.

Earlier, I said that the sixth dimension expands vertically and has various levels, but it also spreads horizontally. What kind of worlds are there in a horizontal sense? First, there is Front Heaven. This area is inhabited by high spirits who have developed their souls as respectable people in an orthodox way. In the sixth dimension, this Front Heaven is what you can truly call the Light Realm.

There are also a few other realms outside of this Front Heaven in the sixth dimension. One example of this is called the Realm of Sea Gods, which has been mentioned in old Japanese tales and legends. It is a part of the Spirit World that has to do with water and is inhabited by many high spirits. The Realm of Sea Gods floats vertically through the different realms of the Spirit World; the major part of it is in the sixth dimension, but it also extends to the fifth and fourth dimensions.

Different kinds of creatures live in the Realm of Sea Gods. Since ancient times it has been said that, in addition to human spirits, creatures such as dragons also exist. Beings called "dragon gods" serve as messengers to the high spirits living in the Realm of Sea Gods. They can exert power over all kinds of natural phenomena or bestow tremendous amounts of energy when required at major turning points in history. Although they are not human spirits, they possess strong spiritual power. That is one of their characteristics.

If you actually see this Realm of Sea Gods, you will find that it is quite vast. It unfolds before your eyes as an ocean of light, and you will feel as if you are living underwater. Taking

Japan as an example, it is geographically connected to Lake Biwa, Miho-no-Matsubara, and the beautiful coastlines near Matsue of the Chugoku region.

Other than the Realm of Sea Gods, there are the Sennin (hermits) Realm and the Tengu (long-nosed goblins) Realm in the Rear Heaven of the sixth dimension. The Realm of Sea Gods is a world of oceans, whereas the Sennin and Tengu Realms are worlds of mountains for the most part. They have steep mountains, and many spirits are undergoing ascetic training mainly on these mountains. The spirits there sought enlightenment while they were alive on earth, but devoted themselves to physical discipline and strove to gain supernatural powers. In other words, the Tengu and Sennin Realms are inhabited by spirits who have attained enlightenment only through the use of psychic powers. These spirits lack human warmth and kindness.

5

Eternal Travelers

I am talking about the sixth dimension based on the concept of evolution. After reading this far, many of you will probably realize that humans are, in conclusion, eternal travelers. But some people may ask, "Why do we have to try so hard to evolve? What's wrong with remaining the way we are now?" In a way, they have a point.

However, if we carefully consider this question from a spiritual point of view, we cannot say that they are right. That is because, in reality, human life is not finite. If human life was something that appears and disappears in the course of 100 to 200 years, maybe humans could stay the way they are now and simply live. But the truth is, humans are essentially spirits that live throughout tens of thousands, hundreds of thousands, millions, tens of millions, or even hundreds of millions of years. If this everlasting life were allowed to stay unchanged, the soul would stop making progress and become stagnant. Not only that, if the soul were to live in stagnation for eons, it would not be able to enjoy real happiness and grow bored. It may be fine to continue doing the same thing for 100 or 200 years, but not for all of eternity; the soul would not want to spend time just floating around idly. As long as humans have individuality and consciousness, they naturally feel they must do something.

Take, for example, office workers. Despite many of them feeling that they want to quit work as soon as possible and live the way they want every day, they nevertheless keep going to work until they retire. When they finally retire and stop going to work, they have too much time on their hands and do not know what to do with it. Although they are free to do what they want every day, they are at a loss because they have no work to do. Most people would not be able to bear living like this for even a year; in less than a year, they would look for another job or immerse themselves in hobbies.

This is due to the essential nature of the soul. The soul is designed to be diligent and not lazy. That is why, although people sometimes want to take time off or slack off, they cannot bear being lazy for long periods. Humans are meant to work. The soul is productive and creative in nature. This is the essential nature of the soul. Many people claim that they do not like to work, but if they were actually deprived of work, they would not know what to do. This is how things are.

The soul is endowed with a level of diligence that urges it to work hard, so it is only natural for humans to strive toward further improvement. No human would be happy just by producing work that is not up to standard. So, people must keep working toward perfection so that their souls can be satisfied, peaceful, and happy. In this sense, the soul or the essence of humans is an eternal traveler. This is the reality.

6

A Diamond in the Rough

Let me further elaborate on the theme of "eternal travelers." Humans aspire to evolve their souls as eternal travelers, but upon hearing this, many people may naturally ask, "Why is there a distinction between high and low spirits? Why are there great figures and not-so-great figures? Why are there the so-called light of guiding spirits and other ordinary spirits? Buddha should love all people equally, so why are there such differences? It doesn't make sense." These questions might come up in your mind, and you may not be able to prevent it.

The answer to these questions lies in the title of this section, "A Diamond in the Rough." Humans were all created as diamonds that shine when they are polished. A diamond that is dug out of a mountain is still in rough form and it is up to each individual, or each diamond, to make it shine. This challenge is assigned to everyone and no one can escape it.

You may compare the light of guiding spirits with ordinary spirits and think, "The light of guiding spirits are diamonds, but we are just pieces of coal or charcoal or stones on a riverside." But that is not true. There is a huge difference between a shining diamond and a stone on a riverside, but that difference is not found in the essence of human souls. The proof of this lies in the fact that anyone can make their soul shine by polishing it.

When people on earth hear about the spirits of hell or devils, they may wonder why such beings exist or think that they should not be allowed to exist. Some of you may even think, "Buddha should just destroy them. Or he should drive them out of this world and out of hell, and confine them to a faraway universe." But that is because you do not yet know the true nature of the soul. In your eyes, the spirits of hell may look very ugly and seem to be always dragging other people into misery. But they, too, can get back on the right track when given the chance.

I have met many people who were possessed by evil spirits and have spoken directly with those spirits. The common trait I find among these spirits is how little knowledge they have of the Truth. They do not know the true nature of the spirit; they do not know that humans are not merely physical bodies; they do not know that they must do good; they do not even know that they are actually in hell. The spirits of hell know nothing of this sort.

But when I tell them the Truth, some of them suddenly come to their senses. Even the so-called evil spirits will wake up and think, "Oh, no. I've been living in the wrong way until now. I shouldn't stay like this. I must live in the right way." In that moment their spiritual bodies, which until then seemed pitch-black, will suddenly emit light. A halo will shine from the back of their heads which were hazy until that time.

Why do they emit the light of a halo? If they were mere stones on a riverside, they would not shine, even after they were polished. But the truth is that, when any spirit polishes its soul, it lights up, which means that even evil spirits or so-called satans were originally created as diamonds. They are diamonds in the rough, and that is why they will shine when polished. It is just that these rough diamonds are covered in soot or mud. Because of this, people usually see them as mere stones and feel like throwing them away, but if you wash them in a river, they will shine brilliantly.

Here lies infinite potential; everyone is endowed with this infinite potential, which is an expression of Buddha's limitless love for us.

7

The Essence of Politics

In this world, many people want to gain power in an earthly sense. Perhaps the most powerful people in this world are politicians, so many people aspire to reach the pinnacle of power, such as by becoming a prime minister, or at least becoming a cabinet minister. They desire power and the ability to rule over others.

But, at the same time, people tend to look down on politicians and politics; they are sometimes disgusted by their strong self-assertion or desire for power. To them, politicians are like arrogant boss monkeys in their own small troops.

Today, people have forgotten much of the essence of politics. The essence of politics lies in its hierarchical relationship; there are the rulers and the ruled, or those with power and those who are controlled. The power pyramid is the essence of politics. Like the shape of a pyramid, there are few people at the top and a large number of people at the bottom. The hierarchy is stable only because it is triangular. If it were circular, it would tumble from one side to the other and lack stability, but it is stable because it is triangular with fewer people at the top.

This hierarchical structure can not only be seen in politics but also in business. The power pyramid exists in companies as well. There are a large number of entry-level workers, or workers without job titles, at the bottom. Then the number of employees decreases as you move up the corporate ladder—for example, from section chiefs to general managers to directors. And in the end, there is only one person at the top—the CEO. The same is true with schools; there are the teachers, then the vice-principal, and then the principal. In the case of universities, they have professors, deans, and then the principal. This pyramidal structure can be found everywhere.

So you need to think about the true reason why things are arranged in this shape. The fact is, the Spirit World is also organized in a pyramidal shape; there are more spirits in the fourth dimension than in the fifth, and more in the fifth than in the sixth. There are fewer spirits as you go higher up and, in the ninth dimension, there are only 10 of them. This is the reality of the Spirit World. In other words, the pyramidal structure is not only found on earth but also in the other world. So we can assume that the power pyramid of this world reflects the structure of the Real World.

Human beings live in communities, and to live harmoniously in communities, it is better to have leaders or governors. If everyone just asserted their opinions, there would be no sense of unity and no one would follow the rules. So there need to be leaders. This is the main purpose of politics.

The spirits of the sixth dimensional Light Realm are striving to improve themselves to fulfill their mission as leaders. They have engaged in a variety of professions but, in essence, these spirits possess the qualities needed to be leaders and are expected to take on leadership roles.

8

Overwhelming Power

I said that the spirits of the sixth dimensional Light Realm take on leadership roles, so now, let us think about why they are able to do so. How can someone make others obey them? What allows someone to give orders or instructions to others? Where does this kind of political power, or perhaps spiritual power, come from?

The truth is that this kind of spiritual power is granted from above. It is the power that comes from Buddha. If Buddha were on the side of hell, justice might lie with the spirits of hell, but it is very clear that He is not. By looking at which side Buddha supports, people can judge which direction is right or which opinion accords with justice. Buddha is like the North Star; He shows people the direction they should head in. That is precisely why those who stand closer to Buddha are allowed to make the people below follow them and fulfill their duties as leaders.

This means that the power of the many leaders in the sixth dimension fundamentally comes from Buddha. Their overwhelming power is essentially the power of Buddha and the wisdom that flows out of Buddha. Without Buddha's power, no one can exert such an overwhelming power on earth or in the other world which is the Real World. What is more, people can display courage and emit brilliance precisely because they believe that their ideas are supported by Buddha.

The spirits of the sixth dimension strongly believe that they are part of the elite chosen by Buddha. They are highly conscious of being among the elite, in a good way. They are fully aware that they have the duty to guide the spirits who are below them, less developed than them, or behind them. There are different ways to guide these lower-level spirits, and the high spirits in the sixth dimensional Light Realm choose their own methods. They study Buddha's Will and Thoughts in a way that is best suited to them and tell others what they have grasped. The sixth dimension is a place where spirits study and explore the Will of Buddha thoroughly.

Based on what they have studied, they guide others with overwhelming power. They say, "From what I have learned, here is Buddha's Will. We must practice politics like this. We must come up with these kinds of economic principles. We must create these types of art. We must provide these kinds of education." They confidently preach this to others.

So, the real source of their power is their knowledge of Buddha's Will. Knowing Buddha's Thoughts is crucial. Knowledge of Buddha's Will, or Wisdom, is the key element of the sixth dimension. Wisdom means knowledge of the Truth, which is the vital factor that allows spirits to live in the sixth dimension. You cannot be in the sixth dimension without acquiring knowledge of the Truth. A condition of being a sixth dimensional existence is to maintain a diligent attitude toward acquiring knowledge of the Truth.

9

Inspiring Words

I have talked about the source of overwhelming power. Now, I would like to move on to the next topic, which is "words." There is a famous verse in the Bible: "In the beginning was the Word, and the Word was with God, and the Word was God" (John 1:1). As you can see from this verse, words are very important. When the light of guiding spirits come down to earth, they essentially persuade and inspire people through their words. Of course, they sometimes perform supernatural phenomena in front of people, but these alone are not enough. Supernatural phenomena are merely an expedient way to guide people toward enlightenment. People cannot attain enlightenment just by experiencing them.

Why is it that people are inspired or moved to begin with? Why are people's hearts shaken when the light of guiding spirits try to persuade them or give sermons, or in modern terms, lectures? Why do people shed tears? We need to know the true reason for this phenomenon.

The reason people in this world shed tears when they hear these spirits talk about the Truth is that deep in their hearts, they have memories of having studied sermons about the Truth in the far distant past. They are recalling these memories. Those impressive memories could be from times when they listened to lectures given by the light of guiding spirits, such as the preachings of Shakyamuni Buddha in India or the sermons of Jesus in Israel. They could also be memories from times they listened to and were moved to tears by the teachings of the light of guiding spirits while they were still living in the Real World—the worlds of the fourth dimension and beyond. This is why people naturally know what is holy.

We do not only cry when we are sad. Tears also well up when we are happy or moved. The tears that flow when we learn the Laws or come into contact with enlightened people, or their words, are known as "the rain of Dharma." These tears have the power to purify people's hearts or their six sense organs that have been defiled by earthly desires. Just as rain falling from the sky washes away the dust in the air, purifies the atmosphere, cleans the earth, and washes the plants and trees, the rain of Dharma or tears wash away the sins in people's minds as they run down their cheeks. At that moment, light will shine forth from their minds. Their minds will emit light just like how a diamond radiates its brilliance.

Religious leaders in the world must provide people with many opportunities to experience the rain of Dharma. While it is certainly important to spread powerful words through writing, it is even more important to talk to people one by one, or give lectures to large audiences, and move them to tears. When people are moved like this, they will be reminded of their real home that is beyond this world and bring out their aspiration for enlightenment once again. They will recall about the time they have been greatly moved by the talks about the Laws or Truth.

The words people use reflect their enlightenment, or how deeply they have understood the Truth. This is the essence of words. That is why, the deeper you attain enlightenment, the more influential and powerful your words will become to move others.

The words of an *unenlightened* person have no power; what they write will not move the hearts of others. On the other hand, if an *enlightened* person writes something similar, it will deeply touch and ignite a flame in people's hearts. This is because their enlightenment is reflected in their writing.

So, if you want to gauge the level of your enlightenment, you just need to see if you can speak about the Truth with inspiring words. You can test yourself in this way. The higher the level of your enlightenment, the more inspiring your words will be and they will emit more light. As a result, your words move the hearts of others. Please use this as a standard to check how far you have advanced in your spiritual discipline.

10

Into the World of Love

In this chapter, I have given an outline of the world of the sixth dimension. Vertically, it has upper, middle, and lower levels, and horizontally, there is the Light Realm in the front, and the Realm of Sea Gods in the middle. Then in the rear, there are the Tengu and Sennin Realms, where spirits who devoted themselves to physical discipline reside. The Tengu Realm is a home for those who mainly like to boast about their power, whereas the Sennin Realm is a home for those who specialized in developing supernatural powers. These kinds of realms exist in the sixth dimension.

I have also explained that many spirits who are referred to as "gods" reside in the sixth dimension. This mainly refers to the spirits of the upper level of the sixth dimensional Light Realm. Various gods live in the upper level, including *Tamonten*, *Bishamonten*, and *Daikokuten*. There are also gods of wealth and other gods. These gods do not necessarily work solely based on sixth-dimensional-level enlightenment. Although some of them have attained the enlightenment of a tathagata (eighth dimensional being) or a bodhisattva (seventh dimensional being), they choose to be in the upper level of the sixth dimension to carry out a particular mission. So, some of the gods in the sixth dimensional Light Realm may have a higher level of enlightenment than sixth dimensional enlightenment. Many of these are tathagatas and bodhisattvas who are in the sixth dimension as commanders supervising spirits of the sixth dimension and guiding people on earth. A large number of them are high spirits who are worthy to be called gods based on their true spiritual grade.

Other than these spirits, there are also those undergoing spiritual discipline in the upper level of the sixth dimension. These spirits are known as *arhats*. Arhats are undergoing spiritual discipline to attain the state of bodhisattvas; they have already cleared the clouds covering their minds, corrected their mistaken thoughts and actions through self-reflection, and have a bright halo. They are at the first stage or the gateway to becoming bodhisattvas. These spirits also live in the upper level of the sixth dimensional Light Realm. In Buddhist terms, they are called arhats. Some ministers and priests of Christian churches have also attained the enlightenment of arhat.

Arhats are those who have completed the part of their spiritual discipline that can be done through self-directed learning. They are making efforts every day with the aim of advancing to yet a higher level, that of a seventh dimensional bodhisattva. They are striving to acquire knowledge of the Truth, while mainly studying how to teach it to others. For them to enter the world of altruism and benefiting others, they must first finish polishing their souls. Then they will be ready to live in a world of fraternity and mercy and of helping and benefiting others with love and mercy. When they reach this point, they will become bodhisattvas. In Christian terms, they will become angels.

These kinds of spirits also reside in the upper level of the sixth dimension. They are on the main road of spiritual discipline. We can say that the spiritual discipline of the sixth dimensional Light Realm is one of the ways to attain the state of arhat, which is one step prior to the stage of bodhisattva. Arhats have established themselves sufficiently in their occupation or their own field. Having done so, they are now aspiring to do the work of helping others, which is their next challenge. These spirits are, in Buddhist terms, arhats. Looking at these traits, we can see that without completing the discipline of the sixth dimension, a spirit cannot advance to the seventh dimension.

The same can be said of the process of spiritual discipline that people living on earth undergo. Only after people have absorbed knowledge of the Truth and put it into practice can they enter the world where they will lead a life devoted to love for the first time. People must clearly understand that without absorbing the knowledge of the Truth, they cannot become bodhisattvas.

So, first, a person needs to absorb knowledge of the Truth and have enough intellectual capability. Then, to make their love more universal, they need to help others and strive to save others with the power of enlightenment. This path is, as we can see from the structure of the other world or the Real World, the right path to follow.

CHAPTER FOUR

The World of
the Seventh Dimension

1

Love Overflows

I will now move on to talk about the realm of souls of the seventh dimension. Another name for the seventh dimension is the Bodhisattva Realm. As you may have noticed, this name has a Buddhist term in it, and not all people across the world understand this term. But I have used this name since it is a familiar expression to those living in Eastern countries like Japan.

In short, the seventh dimension is a world of love. People often speak about love in their daily lives and it has also been the topic of many writings and scriptures of the past. Love is one of the most fundamental desires of human beings and is something that people want to receive at all costs. Everyone wants to be loved by others. But how much they expect to receive and the amount that they actually feel they received will determine their happiness and unhappiness.

Love has been portrayed in many novels and poems, and has been the subject of many philosophies. There is an endless amount of music and paintings about love, too. However, no one in history has been able to describe what real love is and define it perfectly. So I would like to devote this entire chapter to thinking about love from various angles.

I previously said that knowledge is important in the sixth dimension. I also said that this knowledge is not of the mere collection of knowledge from this world but knowledge of the Truth, or Buddha's Truth. And now, I am saying that the world of love exists above the world of knowledge. From ancient times, it has been said that love surpasses knowledge. But this is not to say that knowledge is unnecessary if you have love. It means that, while knowledge is important, what surpasses it is love. We can also see this by looking at what humans have learned through their experiences of love.

There are people who are kind to others and are always willing to help, but often find that they themselves are not happy. Why is that? It is because they are too generous and have a tendency to spoil others. There are many such cases. Some take care of others, almost excessively, out of good intentions only to be resented and feel empty inside. Some devote themselves to others but are neither thanked nor appreciated, and continue to live their life feeling empty. There are a lot of people like this. This happens because they are excessively generous and are spoiling people.

Love seems so simple and easy, but it is very difficult to practice indeed. That is because love needs to be practiced in a way that nurtures others. And to nurture others, you need to deeply understand other people and the world, and know the true nature of the human mind and Buddha's Mind. Without this knowledge, you cannot truly nurture others. So we can say that love backed by knowledge can nurture, guide, and develop everyone in this world, whereas love without knowledge is frail, fleeting, and fragile.

However, if we look deeply into the true nature of the human mind, we will find that love is endlessly welling up from within like a fountain. So I would like you to start by recognizing love as something like a spring that flows out from the depths of our hearts, or the innermost part of our minds.

2

The Functions of Love

Next, let us think about the functions of love. How does love work? To put it differently, what is the purpose of love? What is the role of love? What would happen if love ceased to exist? Is love something that is fundamentally necessary? Or did humans think that love is necessary and decided that they must love each other? We need to consider these points.

After human beings are born from their mother's womb, they have 60 to 70 years of life before they age and die. What is the energy that flows throughout our lives, or the driving force that enables us to live a decades-long life to the fullest? Let us first think about this.

Try looking back on the days when you were a baby crawling around on the floor and then your kindergarten, elementary school, and junior high school days.

Let us first think about what babies do. It seems that their main work is to feel and earn their mother's love. Love is the basic awareness that they first become conscious of. This is an innate ability. When babies feel unloved, they cry; when they feel loved, they look very happy and joyful. When they are given milk or toys, they are happy; when they cannot see their mothers or cannot have things go their way, they cry or scream. When we look at this, we cannot help but notice that babies already display the workings of instinctive love even though they are still pure and innocent. Although they are still very young, they are extremely sensitive and know whether they are being given love or not.

As they grow up and turn three, four, five, and six years old, they become concerned about who among their siblings is loved the most by their parents. When a younger sibling is born, even a four or five-year-old child becomes mischievous when they feel that their parents are giving more love to their younger brother or sister. This is the origin of jealousy. Jealousy begins from an unexpectedly early age.

Looking at how and when jealousy arises, we can see that it stems from a strong desire to be loved. When this desire goes unsatisfied, children will do all sorts of things out of jealousy, such as becoming mischievous or causing trouble for others. It is as though the love that we receive during childhood functions as "food" for us.

As children grow older and go from later elementary school to junior high, and then to high school, they find that love is not only given by their parents but also comes from their peers and teachers. If they are good at their studies, they will be praised by their teachers and win the admiration of their peers. These things will very much satisfy them. Even if they are not good at their studies, they can still attract others' attention and be loved by many for being good at sports. Those who excel in sports or study are often respected and loved by members of the opposite sex. We can say that these kinds of love that children gain function as "nourishment" for them to live by until they reach adulthood.

Then, what about when people reach adulthood? Adults in their twenties start to think seriously about getting married—women wish to be married by 25 or 26 and men between 27, 28, and 30. So that they can be loved by someone of the opposite sex, they study at prestigious schools or go out in society and work hard. Women wear beautiful clothes and makeup and explore ways to make themselves look more attractive. This all comes from the desire to win the love of others.

Looking at these stages of life we can see that, if left as they are, humans are beings that instinctively desire just to be loved by others. But the question is, is such a way of life good enough? Is it really good enough to spend our whole lives from the moment we are born only seeking others' love? We must consider this.

3

The Dynamics of Love

Here, the dynamics of love come into play. In other words, this is about the relationship between one person's love and another's, or the law of action and reaction between the two. We need to consider these dynamics of love.

Everyone craves love when they are a baby. The suppliers of their love are their parents. There is a father's love and a mother's love; the parents act as the suppliers of love and pour out their love and affection on their children. When children grow into adults, get married, and have children of their own, they will then pour out their love onto their children. Children bask in their parents' love. Then, to their grandparents, children are treasures. Their very presence is love and indeed a source of happiness to their grandparents; grandparents are happy just by looking at their grandchildren's faces or holding their hands. This shows that love is not just about receiving; everyone is giving love to each other in one way or another.

From this, you may notice that love is very much something that circulates. In fact, love circulates every 20 to 30 years. Parents give their love to their children, then those children grow up to be parents themselves and give their love to their own children. When they have grandchildren, they will give them love as grandparents. In this way, love goes through a 20 to 30-year cycle.

This is the circulation of love within the family. But humans are faced with a greater challenge of love: the love between men and women. When children reach the age of about 10 and start to become aware of the things around them, they gradually become more conscious of the opposite sex, and from their late teens, their minds become filled with thoughts about the opposite sex. Boys will be thinking about girls and girls will be thinking about boys. Just as how magnets attract each other, they cannot stop thinking about each other all day long. This is a very strange and unexplainable feeling.

What is more, when a man and a woman start dating, they naturally feel loyal to one another as if they signed a contract with each other. The woman instinctively feels, "He loves me so I shouldn't become too close to other men." The same is true with the man. He naturally thinks, "She accepts my love so it would be rude if I get too close to other women." Strangely, this kind of contract-like relationship forms between them. It shows that both men and women know innately that love is something that binds together those who are in love with each other.

Men and women begin to feel love for each other from their teens and into their twenties; they experience the power of love and the binding contract-like nature of it.

These experiences will lay the foundation for marital love to arise in due time. Marital love is protected by law; it is exclusive and does not allow others to intrude into the relationship. From this we can see that love can sometimes be exclusive by nature. If, for example, a husband enjoys his time outside the home and never comes home, his wife will feel very sad. Or, if a wife goes out to have fun and never comes home, her husband will feel very empty inside. As you can see, love contains a desire to be possessive of your partner, which includes a desire to prevent outsiders from intruding in the relationship.

4

Eternal Love

I said that love between men and women, or marital love, has an exclusive and possessive nature. But is being possessive of your partner a type of desire to protect yourself? Should this kind of love be permitted? Let us now think about this point.

Some people may say, "Humans are essentially expected to love all people equally, so we must treat everyone equally." However, what if a wife is equally nice to all men and treats them the same way that she treats her husband? Or what if a husband treats all women in the same way that he treats his wife? What would that mean? It would mean that their marriage would fall apart.

Why are a man and a woman expected to marry and live together? The reason is that by leading a married life, they can have children, raise them, and build a family. But what if building a family was unnecessary? What if men and women only existed for biological reproduction and the government was responsible for raising children, as described in Plato's ideal state? It would mean that the only purpose for men and women to get together is to have offspring.

The truth, however, is that this is not Buddha's Will. Buddha sees that great fruit will be harvested in the process of a man and a woman cooperating for several decades, having children, and creating a happy family. The exclusive and possessive nature found in love between men and women may at first appear like a selfish desire to protect the self. But it is actually the minimum amount of evil needed to achieve a higher purpose, that is, to develop a great family love or to bring about happiness in a family. Being exclusive and possessive may seem narrow-minded, but these feelings are actually working to create something of a higher level.

So, when a man and a woman are in love, it is not necessarily evil to be possessive of the other person. Nevertheless, it is true to say that if this desire becomes extreme to the extent of trying to control the other person and disregarding his or her dignity—more specifically when jealousy becomes too extreme—it will invite unhappiness. Otherwise, we can work on the basis that a "healthy" amount of jealousy is allowed between a man and a woman; that is to say, jealousy that is kept within reason and can serve to protect their marriage is acceptable. Excessive jealousy that makes you overly sensitive and constantly blame and accuse your partner of things will certainly create unhappiness.

We have considered the love between men and women. By letting men and women fall in love, marry, nurture marital love, and practice parental love, Buddha is educating humans about love. In fact, through this love, Buddha is teaching humans that He is love itself.

However, the love between a couple or love between parents and children is not eternal. It is more or less based on instinct. Although the word "coincidence" may not be appropriate, some relationships start and blossom into love by chance. Nonetheless, Buddha has planned for men and women to marry, have children, and build a family together.

But is that all He expects? Of course not. Buddha allows love to develop between men and women so that humans can awaken to real love. No matter how egotistical a person may be, they will have some loving feelings toward the opposite sex, or at least feel affection toward their children. This love toward the opposite sex or one's own family is a step toward understanding eternal love. By experiencing these basic forms of love, a person can awaken to yet a higher level of love—this is the real intention of Buddha. Humans must always remember this.

5

For Whom Do You Love?

We have considered thoughts about love from various angles. Now, let us consider this: "For whom do you love?" In other words, "For whose sake do you love?"

From childhood, humans instinctively learn that it is good when love is given by others but bad when it is not. However, if everyone is on the receiving end of love, no one will be there to supply it. If there was only demand for love and no supply, love would run dry in this world. Even with food, there is not enough supply in the world. Likewise, if everyone only wished to be loved but no one was there to give love, there would be a great demand for love but no supply. This would result in the world being filled with people who are hungry for love.

Love does not only exist between men and women or in a family. When you go out in society, you will see that love can also exist between people outside of a family. It may not be called "love," but people at least care about whether or not they are well thought of by others. We can say that someone who is well thought of by others is someone who is loved. Likewise, we can say that people who think well of others, look after them, and are kind to them are actually giving love to others.

When I look with my spiritual eyes, people living on earth appear like travelers walking through a desert, suffering from thirst and wandering here and there. Under the blazing sun, they wander about the desert saying, "I'm thirsty, I'm thirsty." If only they could love each other, they could quench their thirst, but they cannot because all they think about is receiving love and not giving.

If you contemplate the current situation on earth, you will find an answer to the question, "For whom do you love?" Perhaps you have heard the proverb, "What goes around comes around." It means the things you do for other people will eventually come back to you. In the same way, if you love others, in time the love you give will come back to you.

I would like you all to think about "the economics of love." For example, when a farmer grows vegetables and rice, he will take the harvest to the market, sell it, and then get paid. With the money he earns, he can buy the things he needs. If he buys a car, the man who built the car will earn money, which he can then use to buy vegetables, rice, and so on. In this way, everything is circulating. In our economy, the value created by each person's work or labor is constantly circulating in the form of money. The same is true with love; the love you give will come back to you through other people. You will be given as much as you have given. There is such a law.

For example, with rice, you earn money according to the amount you have grown. In terms of work, you receive a salary according to how much you have worked. Likewise, you will receive the same amount of love that you have given to others. It may not necessarily come back to you in a visible form in this third dimensional world, but from a spiritual perspective, that is exactly what happens. Love will come back to those who give it. This means that the more you give, the more you will earn. That is why spirits in the higher dimensions, or the light of guiding spirits, who love great numbers of people, receive an equally great amount of love themselves.

So, where does the love they receive come from? Does it come as admiration from the people they loved? Yes, that is certainly true, but that is not all. The return or the reward for the love that they give will come from Buddha; it comes as a great blessing from Buddha.

6

True Salvation

Now, let us shift our focus and think about what true salvation is. I said that the seventh dimension is a world of love. I also talked about different kinds of love, such as love within a family, love between parents and children, and love between men and women. So what kind of love do the inhabitants of the seventh dimension mainly have? Seventh dimensional love is obviously not the kind of instinctive love that I just talked about, namely, the love between parents and children or the love between men and women.

When bodhisattvas of the seventh dimension are born into a physical body to live on earth, their main work is to love others, including people whom they do not necessarily have a personal relationship with. With Buddha's Will as their own, they devote themselves to enlightening and saving the people of the world. This is the kind of life bodhisattvas lead on earth and it is what they will continue to do after returning to the other world.

Religions that focus on Other-Power emphasize the salvation movement. They place great importance on saving others or finding salvation. But what exactly is true salvation? Let us think about this point.

I said earlier that when we look at this earthly world with spiritual eyes, it seems as if many weary travelers are restlessly moving here and there in the heat haze of a hot, suffocating desert; they are wandering about in search of water, or an oasis. If people of this third dimensional world are like this, what does salvation mean for them? True salvation is to quench their thirst. We must come to this conclusion.

Then, what is the "water" that quenches their thirst? Two thousand years ago, when Jesus Christ went to a shepherd girl to ask for a cup of water to quench his thirst, he gave the following sermon: "You can quench your thirst with water, but you will be thirsty again. However, those who quench their thirst from the words of life that I give will never be thirsty again."

What he said is true, indeed. Here lies true salvation. What Jesus meant by "the words of life" are the teachings that will truly guide human souls to awaken to eternal life. In other words, it is Buddha's Truth. People who live for the sake of Buddha's Truth have awakened to their eternal life, and that is why they do not become lost, do not tire, and do not thirst.

Countless numbers of weary travelers stood up on their feet after receiving the words of Buddha's Truth that taught them how to live. So, true love, or true salvation, is to offer the words of Buddha's Truth to awaken people and to scold and enlighten them using powerful words. After all, the essence of a bodhisattva's work is to spread the words of Buddha's Truth to protect people's hearts from thirst and to save them.

7

The Lives of Great Figures

I must now touch upon the lives of great figures. There are many great figures in the history of humankind. Of course, not all of them were religious leaders; there were many great people in other fields as well. They lived with love to guide the people of the world and their very existence was love, itself. We must deeply contemplate the lives of such people. They did not only live for the love between men and women, or marital love. Nor did they live just for the love between parent and child. Their way of living showed people that love can even be found in a life that is completely the opposite of living for such kinds of love.

Jesus Christ was one such example. In terms of his love for his parents, he did many things that were considered unfilial and was certainly not a good son. As the son of a carpenter, Jesus was expected to become a skilled craftsman and take over his father's trade, marry and raise children, and support his family for decades. If he had led such a life, he would have been regarded as a good son, but that was not the way he lived.

He was even quite rude to his own mother, who became revered as the Virgin Mary by later generations. He once said to her, "Human souls come from heaven, not from humans.

So woman, although you are the mother of my physical body, in terms of my soul, you are not my mother. Know this." From a worldly perspective, this is a very disrespectful way of speaking to a mother.

Jesus was not really on good terms with his brothers, either. He had four brothers but, unlike Jesus, they were quite ordinary; of all his family, only Jesus was outstanding. His father, Joseph, could not understand him in the truest sense, and neither could his brothers. His brothers would accuse Jesus, saying things like, "What a foolish brother. Instead of helping us and doing the work of a carpenter, he started a new kind of religion and is saying all kinds of strange things."

However, Jesus was living for the love of a higher level; he devoted his life to saving all of humankind. We must know that there is a love that transcends family love, sibling love, and love between parent and child.

The same is true with Gautama Siddhartha or Shakyamuni Buddha. Let us look at his life. He left his home, the Kapilavastu Palace, at the age of 29, abandoned his wife and child, ignored his father's wish, and renounced the world. He then underwent ascetic training in the mountains for six years. As he was born a prince, he was expected to succeed his father as the king, but he cast that aside and left his home. So in a worldly sense, he was quite an unfilial son. He also had a wife named Yashodhara and a son named Rahula, but he abandoned them too; he did not return to Kapilavastu until after he attained Great Enlightenment. In this sense, he was a destroyer of love between men and women, or marital love, and a neglecter of love between parent and child.

However, the real intention of Shakyamuni Buddha was not to deny these kinds of love; this is a fact. Rather, he had to cut off these ties to serve a much higher purpose. If he had continued to live in the palace, he would not have been able to attain Buddha's enlightenment or preach Buddha's teachings to others. It would not have been possible for him to teach the Laws as a prince. In this way, we should not overlook the circumstances of those times. But once he established his group of disciples, he invited his wife and child to join them and looked after them as his disciples. He also accepted many young men and women of his clan—the Shakya clan—into his organization. We must not forget these points. He was, indeed, a man with a strong sense of responsibility.

It may be too much to ask modern people or people of future generations to seek enlightenment even at the cost of their love for their spouse, parents, or children. If possible, a desirable way to practice love would be to save the people of the world while having a harmonious family, taking into account your family environment, parent-child relationships, work, and occupation. This is a universal form of love.

However, we must not forget that among the great figures were people who embodied an exceptional form of love. Their very existence is *love incarnate*, and their lives shine like the sun or stars to guide the way for humankind. This is the truth. Humankind must pay great respect to these people for the lives they led.

8

As an Embodiment of Buddha's Will

We have looked at the lives of great figures in history. In the end, what drove them to go as far as to disregard earthly love was their awareness that their whole life should be dedicated to living for the love of a higher level. They sacrificed something of a lower level for the sake of something of a higher level. This means that their love for Buddha was much greater and deeper than their love for other human beings.

Some people live for the love for others while considering their thoughts and feelings. But the human mind often wavers and changes in various ways. On the other hand, some people live for the love of Buddha, whose Will is eternally unwavering and unchanging. There will certainly be differences in how these two types of people lead their lives.

Your love will truly be eternal and unchanging only when you become an embodiment of Buddha's Will. Only when you live with Buddha's Will as your own, will there exist a true form of love. The love between men and women, between parents and children, and between siblings is not something that should be denied but something to be valued. However, this instinctive form of love is given to humans so that they can prepare themselves for the love for Buddha, which is a higher level of love.

Now, let us think about the love *of* Buddha and the love *for* Buddha.

Buddha embraces humankind with boundless love. This boundless love is not the kind of love that you ask for and be given. It is not a give-and-take form of love, but love that only gives, just like how the sun provides the Earth, as well as all the plants, animals, and humans living on it, with infinite energy and never asks for a penny in return. Similarly, Buddha only gives and continues to shine as love itself, or as the greatest form of love incarnate.

You must be aware of this love from Buddha. You must realize that you have been given so much from Him. You cannot call yourself a child of Buddha unless you appreciate Buddha who just gives so much love. It would be shameful for humans to feel nothing of being given such wonderful love from Buddha each and every day, continuously. It seems that many people in the world pay little respect to the limitless and unconditional love that Buddha gives. Or rather, I think the majority of people are not even aware of what He is giving to them.

However, you need to realize that you are being loved by Buddha and return this feeling of being loved to someone else. When people become adults and have children, they naturally love their children as they were loved by their parents. Buddha is the Father and Mother of humankind. He is the Parent of humankind and, as the Parent, He loves all of humankind without limits. So, I believe humans must give back by passing on this love somewhere else.

What I mean is this: you need to have a deep awareness as a human to live as a child of Buddha. You should not love others out of a desire to receive a good reputation, kind words, or praise; you must give love to others because you are already loved by Buddha infinitely.

When seen with spiritual eyes, human beings receive Buddha's love in the same way that a television antenna receives signals from a broadcasting station. That is why I am saying, "You have already received this much love, so why not pass it on to someone else?" As long as Buddha loves you, you must turn this love into love for other people; you must let it flow throughout the world. It is your duty to let the love you received from higher up the stream flow downstream.

9

Differences in Souls

Now, let us also consider the differences in souls. The human soul can be described as a vessel to receive Buddha's love. If this vessel is small, it will soon fill up, but a large vessel can hold an abundance of Buddha's love. A dam reservoir stores a lot of water and produces electricity by releasing this abundance of water and using the power of the water to turn a turbine. In the same way, every human soul has a "reservoir" unique to their size and generates power according to the amount of "water" that it can store.

The souls that have the largest reservoirs are the saviors in the ninth dimension. They have reservoirs of an unparalleled size that are constantly overflowing with water. Therefore, the water they release from their reservoirs flows downstream with tremendous power and turns the turbine vigorously. As a result, great power is generated, which then circulates throughout the world.

The amount of power that is generated by a reservoir differs according to the amount of water that is stored in the reservoir. In the same way, how much a soul can practice giving love depends on the soul's capacity to retain Buddha's love.

What is more, because hydroelectric power is generated using the power of falling water, the higher the reservoir is located, the further the water has to fall and the greater the energy produced. For that reason, the level of the soul is also important. A soul in a higher dimension, which means a soul with a more noble character, will be able to generate greater power because there is more force to their flow of "water."

Therefore, if you want to develop yourself so that you can receive a greater amount of love, you need to work on "enlarging your vessel" and "elevating your character"—you must put all your energy into working on these two things. To enlarge your vessel, make efforts to be broad-minded. Cultivate tolerance so you can envelop and embrace all things. This is one form of spiritual discipline. Another is to raise the height of the dam, that is, to elevate your soul toward Buddha, one step at a time, through diligent study and work. This effort is none other than spiritual discipline toward enlightenment.

Then, what is enlightenment? What can we define enlightenment as? In fact, enlightenment is the "nourishment of the soul" that you gain by assimilating Buddha's Truth and putting it into practice. The experience and nourishment acquired through assimilating and practicing Buddha's Truth—this is enlightenment. So you need to continuously absorb and study Buddha's Truth and constantly put it into practice; express it in your actions and expand your love in the process. You must increase your tolerance level, elevate your soul, and become a huge "reservoir."

10

What Surpasses Love

We have given various thoughts to the love that runs throughout the world of the seventh dimension. In a way, love is a feeling that works in relation to others; it works between people, between people and animals, and between people and plants. Love is something that is born between the living, and it usually does not exist on its own. A jewel, for example, shines by itself, but love does not work that way. Love is given between people; it is what we give to each other. This is the way love usually works.

Having said that, however, love between the living is not the only form of true love. There is also a love that sheds brilliant light by just existing on its own, like a shining diamond or a crystal glittering under the morning sun. This love surpasses the love that exists between people, between people and plants or animals, and the love for minerals or material objects.

What is it that surpasses love? I must give an answer to this question. What surpasses love is mercy. A diamond shines brilliantly, but that is not because it expects something in return; it simply keeps emitting light. In the same way, there is a greater form of love that shines by itself without expecting anything in return. Love that is given continuously and unconditionally, or the existence of love that is unwavering—this form of love is called *mercy*.

Suppose you are walking in a valley. When you take a rest, you may spot a colorful azalea or violet blooming beautifully among the rocks. Why are violets beautiful? For what purpose do flowers bloom?

Flowers bloom for the sake of blooming—this is their very existence. I believe they are offering us the opportunity to ponder on the significance and value of "existence." Lilies bloom in the valleys for the sake of blooming, and diamonds shine for the sake of shining—here I feel the presence of something that surpasses love. It is not about mutually giving, but is something that only gives, something whose very existence is love itself—this is called mercy. Mercy is valuable even on its own, with or without the existence of others. Mercy transcends love.

After all, mercy is *love incarnate*. It means the very existence of something or someone that is love itself; the very presence of a person that is love for others. This form of love, love incarnate, is a state close to Buddha. Buddha provides love for all beings by just existing. His existence, itself, is love toward all beings. Mercy, or love incarnate, is what surpasses the love that arises between people. This is why all of you are expected to step into the world of mercy.

CHAPTER FIVE

The World of the Eighth Dimension

1

What Are Tathagatas?

In the preceding chapters, I gave an overall picture of the Spirit World up to the Bodhisattva Realm. In this chapter, I would like to move on to describe the Tathagata Realm of the eighth dimension. Like the word *bodhisattva*, *tathagata* is a Buddhist term and it is the equivalent of the Christian term *archangel*. They are also called "light of great guiding spirit."

Let me first define tathagata. The Japanese word for tathagata is *Nyorai*, which means "the one who has come," but where has *the one* come from? It has come from *true thusness*, which means Absolute Truth in Buddhism. So, a tathagata is someone who has come down to this world from a world of indescribably high enlightenment as an embodiment of the Absolute Truth. While it is difficult to give an overall description of the spiritual grade of tathagatas, there is no doubt that they have been, at least, outstanding figures in the history of humankind.

Do you know how many tathagatas there are in total? The total population of the Spirit World is said to be over 50 billion spirits, but only over 400 of them are tathagatas, which means less than 500. That is all. This means that only one out of every 100 million spirits is a tathagata. Therefore, since the population of Japan is currently about 120 million, in terms of probability, there should only be one tathagata in Japan.

But of course, in an age when the Laws that are of a great dimension are being taught, those who are regarded as tathagatas appear in large numbers on earth, so we cannot say exactly how many tathagatas there are in that age. Usually, only a few tathagatas come down to earth in each age, so we would not see tens or hundreds of them take on physical bodies in the same age. That is because the presence of each tathagata is like a huge mountain peak of its own. If, for example, there were high mountains like Mt. Fuji everywhere in Japan, it would be chaotic. Lofty mountains like Mt. Fuji or Mt. Aso give us balanced, beautiful scenery because they stand alone in different places. Likewise, we would not find tathagatas everywhere in the same age. There would usually only be a few of them because they are rare people who stand high and mighty like Mt. Fuji in the time period they are born into.

When a civilization reaches the height of its growth, tathagatas rush to be born into a physical body. One example was the time of Socrates in Greece. Socrates was a tathagata, and so was his disciple, Plato, and Plato's disciple, Aristotle. Around the same time, there was Pythagoras, another tathagata, and quite some time later, there was Archimedes (of the ninth dimension). These tathagatas were born in and around Greece. In ancient China, Confucius (of the ninth dimension), Lao-tzu, and Mo-tzu were all tathagatas. They were the ones who created the ancient Chinese culture.

In Christianity, Jesus Christ was a tathagata (of the ninth dimension), and so was John the Baptist, who heralded the coming of Jesus. Jeremiah and Elijah, mentioned in the history of Jewish prophets, were tathagatas, too. Also, in Buddhism, several tathagatas made appearances—the greatest being Shakyamuni Buddha (of the ninth dimension).

Tathagatas appear on earth to raise the cultural level of the era. They act as a nucleus and teach the Laws, or work to produce a new culture or art, thereby heightening the level of the civilization of their age. As time passes, the culture or civilization they created will eventually decline and bodhisattvas will next appear on earth to restore it. When the restored culture or civilization declines as well, tathagatas will appear again to create something new. Civilizations go through these cycles.

2

The Nature of Light

Those who come to the eighth dimensional Tathagata Realm become fully conscious of light. The word *light* is used in many ways, such as, "Buddha is Light and humans are also light in essence," or "High spirits receive Buddha's Light of Seven Colors and carry out their activities." But what is this light? Is it like a sunray or something similar? I get the impression that people use the word "light" quite often without questioning what it means, so I feel we need to renew our understanding of the light of Buddha and clearly define it.

When we say, "Buddha is Light," what do we mean? One way to define the concept of light is to highlight its qualities by contrasting it with its opposite. The opposite of light is said to be darkness, so let us think about the attributes of darkness. First, we can say that it is visibly dark. Furthermore, obscurity, gloominess, hopelessness, and lifelessness are also attributes of darkness. Light should have the opposite attributes of darkness, so we can say that brightness is one of them. In addition to brightness, it also contains different kinds of will, intention, character, and qualities, which are the source of energy behind all life.

When we talk about light and darkness, we have to face the long-discussed issue of monism versus dualism, that is, the question of whether or not darkness exists in reality. It is true that darkness, in itself, is an absence of something. For example, you cannot radiate darkness to create the night. Darkness only exists because the light is blocked. It exists because of a mediator that is in between. On the other hand, light is a positive existence, an active power.

No matter how strong a particular light may be, if something stands in its way, there will be darkness. And the stronger the light, the darker the shadow. Even the strong light of 10,000 or perhaps a million candela will not reach anyone or anything that is located behind a rock. Light naturally moves directly forward, so if something blocks its way, it will be cut off.

The same can be said of good and evil. Good is a positive existence, whereas evil is a negative or absence-based existence. However, we cannot necessarily say that only good exists and evil does not. Although evil is negative and only exists through an intermediary, it is still there. You could say, "Essentially, there is no such thing as darkness," but where there is light, there is darkness. In the same way, you could say, "Essentially, there is no such thing as evil," but where there is good, there is evil; evil exists to make the good stand out.

While it is true that evil is not a positive existence and is simply a lack of goodness, it is also true that a lack of goodness can make it seem like evil exists. For example, if you illuminate a room with a gigantic fluorescent light or light bulb, there will definitely be shadows somewhere in the room, no matter how bright the light is. Of course, if mirrors were put across the room, there would be no shadows, but in a typical room that people live in, there will be shadows no matter how brightly the room is lit because things like tableware or furniture will block the light. From this, we can say that shadows, darkness, and evil do not exist by themselves. They are natural occurrences in the course of human life.

3

The Essence of Space

In Section 2, I talked about Buddha's light. Now, I would like to go into the topic of *space* while exploring the nature of light further.

What is space in the first place? Humankind has been asking this question for a very long time. Space has length, width, and height, creating three-dimensional space, so space is a three-dimensional box-like cube. We can define space in this way, but it is not entirely correct. Space is not all about length, width, and height because, in reality, the fourth, fifth, sixth, and seventh dimensional spaces exist, as well as the eighth dimensional space which is the subject of this section. This is something we need to take into account.

The truth is that the essence of space is a *field*, which implies that there is consciousness that intends to make something exist within it. What do I mean by a "field"? It is an area of activity where different kinds of phenomena can take place. It is a place where energy runs through and where energy is allowed to carry out its activities. This is what I mean by a "field." A field is a place that is filled with energy and where energy runs through; it is an indispensable area for energy to fully carry out its purpose. This is the essence of space in its true meaning.

So a space is not merely a cube consisting of length, width, and height, but a field that is necessary for Buddha's light to carry out its activities and do all kinds of work. Therefore, the definition of three-dimensional space does not apply to the multi-dimensional space of the fourth dimension and above because the multi-dimensional space is not a cube. It is a space that is created by different consciousnesses where Buddha's light can make many different kinds of phenomena happen and carry out various activities.

4

Eternal Time

Next, I would like to talk about *time*, which is often put in contrast with space. It is often said that space and time expand in different directions; space expands horizontally whereas time extends vertically. But if there was no time, would there still be space? How are time and space related to each other? We need to consider these points, too.

Earlier, I defined space as a field that is created for light to carry out its activities. When light carries out the activities of light, there will be movement of some kind, which implies that there is also a flow of time. Then, what would space mean if time were to stop? Could light still move if time stopped? The answer is that if time stops, light will also freeze, just like how it appears when captured in a photograph.

For space to fulfill its original role as a domain for light to carry out its activities, it must contain time. In other words, space cannot exist without time. You cannot separate time and space; time allows space to exist as space. The condition for light to carry out its activities is that the field, in which light is located, continues to exist.

You must not think of light as a mere ray or beam. Light can be broken down into minute particles, the smallest of which is called a *photon*. These photons combine to form tiny particles that ultimately make up all physical creations, including the human body. So all material things are made of light. When light solidifies and takes on form, it becomes a material object. On the other hand, light that has not solidified exists as a spirit, or spiritual energy, in the fourth dimensional space and above. This means that everything in this world—in this third dimension as well as in the fourth dimension and above—is created from light; the truth is that everything *is* light.

Since everything is made of light and given that space is a field where light carries out its activities, it would mean if there was no place for light to carry out its activities, there would be no space. From this, we can see that "light" and "the activity of light" are the two elements that make up the multi-dimensional space of the third dimension and beyond. This means that, if it were not for time, which allows light to carry out its activities, there would be no space, no material objects, no spirits, nothing. Instead, there would just be something like a floating mirage; it would not be a space for light to be active in. The reason space exists is for light to carry out its activities within it, so we need to understand time as a crucial factor that allows space to exist.

As we think about this, we will come to understand that the world Buddha created, that is to say, the world of the third, fourth, fifth, sixth, seventh, and eighth dimensions, consists of space that contains time and light that moves within it. So, the elements with which Buddha created the world come down to these: light, space, and time. Buddha created the world with these three elements: *light*, which can change itself to become the material and spiritual bodies of various dimensions; *space*, which is necessary for light to exist as light and be active; and the flow of *time*, which is also necessary for light to carry out its activities—for light to flow as light and for light to reach somewhere, there must be a flow of time. Thus, light, space, and time are the three elements with which Buddha created the heavens and the earth. This is what we should know.

5

Guideposts for Humankind

When you understand the true nature of the world that humankind lives in, the answers to why humankind is allowed to live on earth, how human life is sustained, how humans should live, and what the purpose of life is will be revealed. Understanding the overall picture of the world that Buddha created and seeing its true nature will lead you to discover the guideposts for human beings to live by.

What are the guideposts for human beings to follow when living their lives? You will discover them once you become aware that humankind is being allowed to live in a world that Buddha created with light, space, and time, and once you perceive Buddha's intention for creating such a world.

So, what kind of world did Buddha intend to create using the three elements of light, space, and time? Let us imagine space to be a transparent glass box. When light shines into it from one corner of the box, it will move around inside the box by reflecting off the walls. The light reflects off one wall to the next, then onto the next, and so on; light continuously travels around inside the box. Being trapped inside the box, the light will move in all sorts of ways and create all kinds of scenery—an artwork of light. When we look at the history of the universe and humankind in terms of this glass box, we realize that light is not being allowed to exist by chance, but is following a purposeful course. In other words, light emitted by the Primordial Buddha governs the evolution of the universe and humankind. It was not emitted at random but with clear objectives.

The objectives of Buddha's light for carrying out its activities can be roughly summarized into two points.

The first objective is evolution. If we look at the universe, Earth, and the history of Earth and the history of humankind, we will discover in all of them that the great purpose or objective is evolution. This is an undeniable fact. Because humankind is seeking something of a higher level, it is allowed to live and that is precisely why there is value in humans to keep on living. If humankind lived just to degenerate, then we would need to question the purpose of its existence.

Why should humankind exist at all if it is simply meant to degenerate? When we work with clay, for example, it gives us great joy to create an object out of something that has no form. But if animals such as elephants, monkeys, or humans were made of clay and were living only to return to blocks of clay, their lives would be completely meaningless. The essence of evolution is to transform from something *without* form into something *with* form. For something without form to develop into something with form, and then to develop into something even more wonderful—evolution of this kind is one of the objectives of humankind.

Another objective is harmony; to create grand harmony or great harmony. What do I mean by great harmony?

Let us imagine that Buddha created a mountain of clay in an infinitely vast room. From this clay, He made the Sun, the Earth, the Moon, then plants, animals, people, and all kinds of other things. It is a wonderful thing to have something formless evolve into something with form. But the next issue would be how each of these beings that He created could co-exist in an orderly and beautiful way. There is the ratio of plants and animals to human beings; the appropriate positioning of the solar system—the Sun, the Earth, the Moon, other planets—and other stars; and the right ratio of day to night, land to sea, and hot to cold. The harmony of all these things would be the next issue that Buddha would consider.

Thus, we can say that the history of humankind has been unfolding with two major objectives, which are progress and harmony, or evolution and harmony.

6

What Are the Laws?

I have said that the guideposts for humankind boil down to evolution and harmony. What, then are the Laws that people seek and explore? What is the Truth? What are the Laws, which are the systematic teachings of the Truth and what role do they fulfill?

The Laws are the rules that govern the universe and the systematic teachings of the Truth. They contain the two elements of evolution and harmony that I talked about earlier, which are the objectives of the Laws.

The Laws certainly contain the element of evolution that helps every person make improvements. There have never been Laws of Truth or Buddha's Laws that do not guide humans to improve, and nor will such Laws be allowed to exist in the future. The principles of progress and evolution are inherent in the Laws. Therefore, the Laws must include teachings that work to enhance the maturity and enlightenment of individuals and improve each person.

While it is good for each individual to make progress, sometimes the freedom they exercise causes conflict to arise with other people. For this reason, we also need Laws to help improve our communities which are made up of individuals.

Let us say that a man wants to become the CEO of the company he works for, but he is not the only one who wants the position. Suppose two other people also feel the same way. Not all three of them can become CEOs at the same time, so the members of the board will begin considering who is best suited for the position. They will consider who, among the three candidates, has the best leadership qualities to lead hundreds or thousands of employees as their CEO. If only one of them possesses such qualities, the board will appoint him to be the next CEO and decline the other two. In this way, the principle of coordination will come into play. If all three candidates are suitable for the post, the board will need to coordinate and decide the order that the three men will serve in the position, for example, Mr. A, Mr. B, and then Mr. C.

As seen in this example, we need a set of rules or principles that coordinates each individual's self-improvement and progress for the benefit of the whole. This is why there have been various religious leaders, moralists, and philosophers who taught the laws on the principles of coordination and harmony. For example, Confucius, who appeared in China and taught Confucianism, presented the seniority system as the principle of coordination. He taught that precedence should be given to older people and that younger people should respect their elders. This means that, if the three candidates from the example are equal in terms of their abilities, they will become the CEO in the order of their age. This idea still exists in some countries today, to an extent. Although a person's age does not necessarily indicate the maturity of their soul, people assume that a person with more experience has more wisdom compared to those who are younger and have similar abilities. The seniority system is based on this kind of assumption.

Of course, other perspectives are also needed. One example is the merit system. Under this system, you may have to take examinations or have your past achievements compared to those of others, and the person with the best results will be at the top. So, the merit system acts as another yardstick. There is also the idea of utilitarianism, for example, as put forward by Jeremy Bentham. It advocates for "the greatest happiness for the greatest number of people" or making a choice that will serve to benefit the most people. It is another possible way. John Stuart Mill also supported this idea.

In the end, the progress that individuals achieve should be returned to society so the whole of society can progress. We need the principle of coordination for this reason. This idea is the Law that encompasses the philosophies of both the Small Vehicle (Hinayana) and the Great Vehicle (Mahayana) of Buddhism. That is, the principle of progress is essential as a way for an individual to attain enlightenment

(Hinayana), whereas the principle of coordination is essential in order to create Buddha Land utopia in this world (Mahayana). The fundamental principles of these Laws are the two major principles—progress and harmony. Only when these two are well-balanced can the happiness of all humankind be realized.

7

What Is Mercy?

Let me now talk about the Laws and mercy. The teachings of Happy Science are based on the principle of progress for individuals and the principle of harmony for society as a whole. Based on these two principles, I teach that it is the innate nature of humans to pursue happiness and that the happiness that humans should seek and pursue comprises both private happiness and public happiness. Seeking private happiness means seeking the happiness of the individual. On the other hand, seeking public happiness means expanding the private utopia that a person has achieved as the result of seeking the happiness of the individual to the whole of society, the world, and all of humankind. This will lead to the realization of a public utopia. In fact, Happy Science bases its activities on these principles.

Now, the question is, why do we need to seek and pursue these two kinds of happiness—private happiness and public happiness? We need to consider whether there is a guiding principle behind them.

As I said, it is the innate nature of humans to seek happiness. This is a nature that Buddha has bestowed on humans out of His Mercy. It is a purpose that Buddha gave to humans to live by. If this purpose were to make humans unhappy, then the world would be a terrible place. However, the truth is that Buddha imbued human souls with the desire to seek happiness. That is why humans naturally strive to be as happy as they can. So we must understand that this nature to seek happiness is embedded in our soul, which is our real entity and what makes us human beings.

The fundamental reason humans naturally seek happiness is that they are children of Light who have branched off from the Primordial Buddha. The fact that humans are children of Light or children of Buddha means that they have the same nature as Buddha.

What is the nature of Buddha? Buddha approves of a greater sense of happiness generated through both progress and harmony because He, Himself, is the energy of happiness. Buddha supervises, governs, and prevails over the Great Universe as this energy. So, we can conclude that the reason Buddha exists as Buddha, or the very purpose of His existence, is in happiness; this is Buddha's foundation.

What, then, is happiness for Buddha? When does Buddha feel happy? He finds joy when all of His creations develop and prosper while realizing great harmony. It is in this very process of their birth, growth, development, and prosperity that Buddha discovers joy. If Buddha was motionless, there would be no joy. But when Buddha carries out His activities as Buddha with the goal of bringing development and prosperity to all while realizing harmony, then in that process, He gains a magnificent, beautiful experience that comes with joy. Through this experience, Buddha also transforms, expands, and develops to become an even greater existence. Buddha created humans in a way that they instinctively pursue happiness and can live happily. This, in itself, shows the nature of Buddha, or His Mercy.

8

The Functions of a Tathagata

In this section, let us think about the functions of a tathagata, or the role and work that tathagatas fulfill. In *The Laws of the Sun*, I described that Buddha created all human souls equally; what is more, not only does He see humans from the perspective of equality, but He also sees them from the perspective of fairness and evaluates them according to the work they do. Fairness implies that those who guide many people will be given an appropriate position, role, and suitable power. The state of tathagata—a much higher state than others—is supported by this principle of fairness.

All souls started out equal in how they branched off as Buddha's children. As they go through many reincarnations, however, some among them acquire great wisdom. These souls are then placed in suitable positions to let them pursue even greater self-realization. This is Buddha's intention.

When we think about the functions of tathagatas from this perspective, we can say that they are, in essence, representatives of Buddha. Buddha is not a being like humans who have hands and feet and can be seen moving around. Buddha is the Being who created the Great Universe, which is a vast, multi-dimensional space, so it is impossible for humans to see or touch Him. That is why tathagatas exist as great beings that allow people to feel the presence of Buddha. In other words, tathagatas exist so that people can get a sense of Buddha Himself. This is the fundamental reason why tathagatas are the embodiment of love incarnate.

Tathagatas are beings who "came from the Truth," and they are the embodiment of the Absolute Truth. This means that their very presence is love for human beings. In other words, tathagatas are those who ceaselessly strive to awaken humans, enlighten them, and invite them to a state of happiness. So, we can say that tathagatas are Light itself and are a personification of Buddha.

Humans cannot see, understand, or fully grasp Buddha Himself, but they can at least imagine what Buddha is like through the presence of tathagatas. Tathagatas exist as role models for humans so that they can imagine Buddha and how merciful He is. Although humans cannot see Buddha directly, they will gradually be able to feel His Great Mercy and His Greatness by observing tathagatas. After all, tathagatas exist for the purpose of educating others. Their very being, in and of itself, has the function of educating many people or all people.

9

Talking about Buddha

Ultimately, the role of a tathagata is to speak about what Buddha is. Tathagatas are Buddha's representatives or spokespeople who are allowed to talk about Buddha. Ordinary people do not have the authority to speak about Buddha, of course, but because tathagatas are much closer to Him than ordinary people are, they are allowed to do so. Beings of the eighth dimension are permitted to speak about Buddha as the light of great guiding spirits.

However, even eighth dimensional tathagatas are not allowed to speak about Buddha entirely. This is because Buddha is so great and His characteristics encompass so many things, that it is impossible for a single human soul to teach them all. For this reason, in the eighth dimensional Tathagata Realm, various tathagatas are working as leaders, each of them representing one of the colors of spiritual light that appear through the Prism of Buddha.

Tathagatas under the yellow light, or golden light, whose supreme leader is Gautama Siddhartha, focus mainly on the aspects of enlightenment, the Laws, and mercy when describing Buddha. Tathagatas under the light of love, or the white light, which is governed by Jesus Christ, talk about Buddha from the perspective of love. Tathagatas of the red light that is governed by Moses try to reveal to people what Buddha is through miracles, which Buddha can make happen.

There are also other colors of light. The green light, as represented by the philosophies of Taoism, teaches about the great harmony of Mother Nature. Tathagatas who receive the green light are there to teach that Buddha exists in the harmony of nature where everything is in its natural state. They do so by referring to Mother Nature and its great harmony. Zeus is in charge of artistic activities, and tathagatas who are active as artists convey to people what Buddha is through the spiritual light of art. Those under the stream of the purple light, which is governed by Confucius, teach obedience, order, and loyalty; through these qualities, they teach that feelings of awe and respect are necessary on the road to Buddha. In this way, they let people take a glimpse into what Buddha is.

Tathagatas essentially speak about Buddha from the viewpoint of the spiritual light they belong to. This is the correct way to understand the teachings of tathagatas. However, humankind did not know that there are various colors of light with different characteristics, or that each tathagata taught the Laws from the viewpoint of their own stream of spiritual light. So, for a long time, humans have been engaged in religious conflicts and wars. People have gotten into conflict after labeling others as heretics if they had different roles or believed in different descriptions of

Buddha or God. They have regarded other religions as evil and wrong. But what humans must now do is to look at the work of the various tathagatas who are under different spiritual light and try to know the truth about Buddha.

10

The Road to Perfection

Now, you may wonder, "Are the spirits of the eighth dimensional Tathagata Realm completely done with their soul training? Is there no further spiritual training for them?" Let us consider this point.

The truth is that even tathagatas who are born on earth with physical bodies are still undergoing spiritual training as human beings. Spirits in the eighth dimension are specialists and great beings who embody different colors of spiritual light. But as they reincarnate from the other world to this world once every several hundred or several thousand years, they see and hear many things and gain various kinds of experiences. By leading lives on earth, they also learn things that are different from what they think is most important and become familiar with teachings that belong to the colors of spiritual light other than their own. In this respect, we can say that even tathagatas are still in the process of spiritual training toward enlightenment. Even so, we cannot deny the fact that they are much closer to perfection than other souls.

So what is the road to perfection that tathagatas are taking by undergoing soul training? The answer is that, through their spiritual discipline, they are devoted to gaining a grander integrated viewpoint; or in other words, an all-encompassing view of human beings, the teachings, and the history of Earth and humankind. Simply put, the purpose of their spiritual training is to gain an even higher level of awareness and insight. In this respect, we can say that tathagatas, too, are undergoing spiritual training to develop their awareness and insight.

Buddha has made it a rule for humankind to undergo the cycle of reincarnation so that humans can evolve and make progress. No spirit is exempt from this rule. But it is often said that tathagatas are emancipated from the requirement to reincarnate or that a condition of being a tathagata is being free from the cycle of reincarnation. So let me explain the meaning behind these ideas.

The truth is that even tathagatas cannot go without reincarnating for thousands, tens of thousands, or hundreds of thousands of years. They actually do reincarnate on earth, but they choose to do so and make a plan to be born at various times at their own will. In contrast, those in the Bodhisattva Realm and below are sent to live on earth as a requirement. They are required to be born in a certain age as part of their compulsory education. Tathagatas are souls who have completed their compulsory education. But if they want to study further, they can do so as they like, in the same way that people in society continue to learn even after becoming adults.

Having finished their compulsory education, tathagatas continue to learn on their own accord aiming for an even higher goal. Moreover, they are granted the freedom to choose what they learn. The purpose of their learning is to gain a higher awareness and insight which will allow them to see things from a more global and universal point of view. Thus, we can say that tathagatas are spirits who are undergoing great spiritual discipline for this purpose and are walking the road to perfection.

CHAPTER SIX

The World of
the Ninth Dimension

1

The Other Side of the Veil

In chapters one to five, I described the structure of the worlds from the fourth dimension to the eighth dimension, as well as the rules that govern these worlds. I do not think there have been many documents throughout history that unveiled the world after death in such detail as I have done in these chapters.

And now, I would even like to go further in this book and explore and analyze the world of the ninth dimension. To philosophers and religious leaders throughout the ages, the ninth dimension has always been a world that is on the other side of the veil. In other words, I intend to describe this realm that has remained a mystery and unknown to this day, in a way that can be understood by humans.

The world of the ninth dimension that lies behind the veil is namely, a world of saviors. The spirits of this realm are saviors or messiahs who only come down to earth once every few thousand years, or even less often than that.

On Earth, there are various civilizations and ages. So, in a particular age, there will be ninth dimensional beings that are born on earth while some that are not. In other words, some of them will be born once every 2,000 or 3,000 years in that particular age, while others will not appear at all.

Put simply, the spirits of the ninth dimension decide which role each of them will play in an age and decide who among them will lead the activities. This produces the distinctive characteristics of a civilization or age.

The most famous saviors to appear in the current civilization are Gautama Siddhartha (Shakyamuni Buddha), Jesus Christ, and Moses. Confucius, who was born in China, is not usually referred to as a savior, but he is also an inhabitant of the ninth dimension, the world of saviors. The common trait shared by these figures is that they have established the principles of civilizations for humankind.

2

A Mystical World

The ninth dimension is a very mystical realm. I cannot generalize about how everybody on earth imagines the other world to be. But one thing I can say is that, essentially, the spirits of the ninth dimension have almost become non-human existences. This is a fact.

The inhabitants of the fourth dimensional Astral Realm practically live in the same way they did when they had a physical body, although they are now spiritual entities. Spirits in the fifth dimensional Goodness Realm retain the senses they used to have as human beings. Many of them take on occupations that are found on earth. For example, some are working as carpenters, schoolteachers, store clerks, machine manufacturers, and so on. There are also many who are engaged in agricultural work. In the fifth dimension, a large number of earthly occupations still exist and a lot of spirits are working accordingly. So, the fifth dimension is a world that you can understand through the human senses.

In the sixth dimensional Light Realm, the inhabitants have a higher level of awareness. They shine so brilliantly that they would make you think of divine beings. Even so, they still take on a human form, with hands and feet, in their daily lives. But from time to time, they remember that they are actually consciousnesses and act accordingly. An example of what I mean by this is that the spirits of the sixth dimensional Light Realm can fly wherever they want to go. Spirits with a Western background may do so by taking the form of an angel with wings on their back. Other spirits may take an Eastern approach and travel around by riding on clouds, just like how the Monkey King (Sun Wukong) traveled on his magic cloud in the novel, *Journey to the West*. They can do such things. So, the spirits of the sixth dimension sense things in a slightly different way from how humans do on earth with their five sensory organs.

What about the Bodhisattva Realm of the seventh dimension? Bodhisattvas are still undergoing much spiritual discipline in human form, but a large part of their work is also to educate and guide other spirits who are still developing themselves. So the majority of them are not just living peacefully and comfortably in the seventh dimensional Bodhisattva Realm; rather, they visit the sixth, fifth, and fourth dimensions to do all kinds of work and, as guiding spirits, they guide the people on earth to make the world a better place.

The spirits in the seventh dimension are more freely engaged in a wide range of activities, and in this sense, their lifestyle is no longer the same as humans. They have a much higher degree of self-awareness and self-recognition. Nevertheless, even in the seventh dimension, when bodhisattvas want an objective view of themselves, they would try to remember the human form that they had when they lived on earth, with a head, hands, and feet, and understand who they are through it.

However, things are a little different in the eighth dimensional Tathagata Realm. Tathagatas of the eighth dimension also come to earth from time to time to guide religious leaders as guiding spirits and, when they do, they appear in the form of divine, godlike existences.

But that is not to say that they retain that form in the other world. They are at a stage where they no longer need to take on a human form. When tathagatas talk to each other and exchange ideas, they may take on a human appearance to make it easier for them to recognize each other, but that is not how they usually are. Most of the time, they do not have a human form. Actually, they can freely split themselves into more than one entity or transform themselves into something else.

Tathagatas can have parts of their own consciousnesses do various things. In *Journey to the West*, when Monkey King plucks out one of his hairs and blows on it, it turns into an elephant or copies of himself. The eighth dimension is such a world; by using different parts of their consciousness the inhabitants can carry out many kinds of activities. They can split themselves into many beings of light, all with the same purpose.

This is how things are up to the eighth dimension, but the ninth dimension is a far more mystical realm and difficult to understand from the theories and senses of this earthly world. Although I said that ten spirits reside in the ninth dimension, it does not mean that there are ten human spirits. The most suitable way to describe these existences is that there are ten gigantic pillars of light, each with unique characteristics. When they communicate with me on earth, they take on a human appearance and the personality they used to have when they were alive, but that is not their usual form.

It is very difficult to describe these existences, but let me try using electricity as a metaphor. We could say that there are ten batteries each with unique characteristics in the ninth dimension. Each battery has a wire attached to its positive and negative terminals with different light bulbs in between. When an electric current flows through the wire, the bulbs light up. Each of these bulbs has a different name, for instance, Ra Mu, Rient Arl Croud, Hermes, or Gautama Siddhartha. Although there may be several light bulbs, they are all connected to the same battery. An electric current just flows through the wire, and when necessary, the bulbs will light up to express their unique characters.

3

The Truth about the Spirits of the Ninth Dimension

So what is the true nature of the "gods" who reside in the ninth dimension? You might imagine them to be sitting on a large throne in a palace, wearing a long, white robe and a crown as depicted in old tales, but that is not the case. Ninth dimensional beings are actually electromagnetic waves, energy bodies, or consciousnesses, and this is the form they take when they carry out their work. When a part of their consciousness is active, like a light bulb that is lit up, people recognize it by its distinct figure and light.

Take, for example, the soul of Jesus Christ. Jesus is a ninth dimensional being, but this is not to say that he lives in the ninth dimension looking like Jesus on the cross with a thin body, beard, and long hair. He exists as a mass of light with Jesus' characteristics. And whenever necessary, it is this light that guides people on earth and spirits of the eighth dimension and below. When Jesus appears in front of the tathagatas of the eighth dimension or bodhisattvas of the seventh dimension to guide them, he takes on the form he had on earth because that makes it easier for them to recognize him. Even so, only spirits in the eighth, seventh, and perhaps sixth dimensions can see him. To those of the lower dimensions, he simply looks like a mass of light; he is too bright for them to see even if he appears in human form. So the inhabitants of the lower dimensions do not know what he looks like.

This is because there is quite a difference in the amount of light between Jesus and the spirits of lower dimensions. I have talked a lot about the differences between each dimension in the other world, but essentially, the difference is in the amount of light that the consciousnesses of each dimension have. Light, here, does not mean a simple light but a light with certain characteristics. There are different-colored bundles of light—bundles of yellow light, white light, red light, green light, and so on. This is the reality of light. Of course, I am only using words such as yellow, white, red, and green to make it easier for people on earth to understand. In truth, there are not even such things as colors of light.

In fact, there is no such thing as color on earth, either. Something that seems to have a blue color is actually only reflecting the blue light within the sun's spectrum. An object that absorbs all of the sunlight appears black, whereas an object that reflects all of it appears white; if it reflects only the yellow light it will appear yellow. So an object essentially has no color; it simply means the particles that make up the object are reflecting a certain color of light in the sun's spectrum, thereby making it look colored. You will understand that color essentially does not exist when you turn off the light; without light, there is no color. If colors really existed, they would glow in the dark, but whether an object is red, white, or yellow, it has no color in the dark. The truth is that what we think of as colors are simply reflections of certain wavelengths of light. Because of this, there is no color when there is no light. In reality, objects have no color; it only looks like there are colors when certain wavelengths of light are being reflected.

4

The Essence of Religion

In this section, let us consider the essence of religion. In my description of the eighth dimension, I said that Buddha's light is split into a spectrum as if passing through a prism, and the teachings that are preached are characterized by each type of light. And I explained that what tathagatas taught as their own ideas of Buddha (or God) became the source of each religion.

But why is it necessary to have different teachings? Some people may think, "It would be better if we just had one idea that represented Buddha's teachings. All religious leaders should teach the same thing based on that idea. Then, there would be no confusion or religious wars, and people would not have trouble choosing a religion to believe in."

However, I find danger and something wrong with this way of thinking. The question is, "Would humans be satisfied with a 'one-size-fits-all' religion?" Even with cars, for example, people drive all kinds of cars. There are a variety of car brands and they come in different colors, such as white, red, yellow, and blue. The car size also differs—large, medium, and small. There are differences in the degree of fuel efficiency and price as well, and furthermore, there are brand-new cars and used cars. Everyone chooses a car that suits their needs or their family's needs.

Why is there such a wide variety of cars? It is because cars are not just a means of transporting people or goods. If cars were merely tools to take people from one place to another, it would not matter if they all looked the same. Cars must play another role.

What is this role? The answer is that they symbolize many things. For example, cars symbolize the owner's financial or social status. They also represent the owner's preferences. They reveal whether the owner is someone who is practical or someone who sees cars as a status symbol. We can find out many things about someone from the type of car they own. Furthermore, some cars appeal to men whereas others appeal to women. Speed can also be a factor. Some people prefer to drive slow cars rather than fast cars like the ones professional racers drive. Design also matters; some like two-door cars whereas others prefer four-door or five-door cars. Therefore, if you were asked which car is the best, you would not be able to choose one car that suits all people.

Likewise, there are many religious groups in the world today. Trying to pick the most righteous one is the same as asking which car is the best. Of course, we can say in general that the more expensive the car, the better it is, or that certain cars are more luxurious than others. But this does not necessarily mean that everyone must ride a particular car. What people prefer varies from person to person.

In Buddhism, there are the terms *Hinayana* and *Mahayana*. *Yana* means "vehicle." Hinayana means "Small Vehicle" and Mahayana means "Great Vehicle." Hinayana is like a small car that can carry only one person, whereas Mahayana is like a large car that can carry many people. So, there are "small cars" and "large cars" in religion, and the difference between them lies in the amount of people they can carry. For instance, no one would want to drive a bus for their everyday errands because, although a bus can carry a large number of people, it is not suitable for individual use. Just as there are vehicles of different sizes, there are different kinds of religious teachings, like Hinayana and Mahayana, to suit people's tastes and the climates and environments they live in.

Therefore, in the desert regions of the Middle East where conflicts and destruction were prevalent, God needed to appear as the "God of Judgment" to teach people justice, whereas in the temperate region of the Orient, God needed to teach harmony. At times, in order to create a modern, rational civilization like the current Western civilization, God's teachings were given in the form of philosophy. Whatever form God's teachings may take, their objective is always the same—to transport people from point A to point B. Various "vehicles" are prepared as the means for humans to travel from one point to another, and they can find joy and the meaning of life by "riding" them. This is what has been planned for humans.

5

The Seven Colors Split through the Prism of Buddha

It is said that Buddha's light is made up of seven colors, and this is indeed true. In the ninth dimension, Buddha's light is split into seven colors, which are then further divided into more than ten or twenty different colors by the tathagatas in the eighth dimension and sent down to the dimensions below.

Here, let me name the ninth dimensional Grand Tathagatas who are in charge of each of the seven colors.

The central color yellow—or gold—is under the command of Gautama Siddhartha, otherwise known as Shakyamuni Buddha. Buddha's yellow light is the color of the Laws or mercy.

The white light is under the command of Jesus Christ. Jesus' white light is the color of love. The group of spirits who work in the medical field draw on this white light of Jesus. I am not sure whether it is a coincidence that doctors and nurses wear white, but it is as if they are implying that they belong to the white light group.

Moses is responsible for the red light. The red color is the light of leaders; it guides the leaders who govern a society, such as political leaders. This light is also referred to as the light of miracles. When miracles or inexplicable phenomena occur, the red light is at work.

Then there is also the blue light. Put simply, blue is the color associated with philosophy and ideology, and is controlled not by one spirit but two. One is Zeus, who once lived in ancient Greece. When he lived as Zeus, he mainly governed literature and the arts. The spiritual light of the arts belongs to the green light, but part of the arts is also governed by the blue light. The other spirit who is in charge of the blue light is Manu. In India, he is referred to as the progenitor of humankind; his philosophy became the basis of the "Laws of Manu" (or Manu Smriti), which outlined the daily conduct of the Brahmins. He is a spirit of the ninth dimension and mainly deals with ideological matters, but is also actively carrying out special missions that are assigned to him. At present, he is in charge of matters such as racial issues and is working to integrate different ideologies and beliefs across all regions.

Other than these colors, there is the silver light, which is the light of science and the light of modernization of civilizations. The ninth dimensional tathagata who splits this light is Isaac Newton. A part of Newton's spiritual entity was previously born as Archimedes in ancient Greece. He is always a scientist when born on earth; as a ninth dimensional tathagata, he is in charge of one of the colors of Buddha's light and is responsible for the advancements in science in the third dimension and above. Scientists such as Thomas Edison and Albert Einstein in the eighth dimensional Tathagata Realm are working under the stream of Newton.

There is also the green light, which mainly governs harmony. Green is the color of the philosophies of Taoism, and it is the color of Mother Nature and harmony. The spirits who are in charge of this color are Manu, whom I mentioned earlier, and Zoroaster (Zarathustra), a god who appeared in the Near and Middle East and taught Zoroastrianism or fire worship, which is based on the dualism of good and evil. They mainly teach the way of Mother Nature, the structure of the universe, and the harmony of the universe.

Another color is the purple light, which is the light of Confucius who appeared in China. He mainly preaches morality, the academic ways of thinking, obedience, and order. In other words, Confucius takes on the purple light to govern hierarchical relationships and maintain order. The gods of Japanese Shinto are under the influence of this light.

I have introduced the eight Grand Tathagatas who are in charge of the seven colors of Buddha's light, but as I have already said, there are ten Grand Tathagatas in the ninth dimension. So who are the other two and what do they do? I need to talk about this, too. One of the two is Enlil. He has also been known as Yahweh in the desert regions of the Middle East. He has fulfilled his role as the ethnic god of the

Israelites, but in the Orient, he is feared as the head of the "gods of vengeance." The other spirit is Maitreya, whose role is to work as a coordinator. He is responsible for dispersing Buddha's light into a spectrum and is in charge of adjusting the intensity of each light—in other words, which light to intensify or which light to weaken.

6

The Work of Shakyamuni Buddha

The central being of the ninth dimension is the spiritual entity whose part was once born in India as Gautama Siddhartha, otherwise known as Shakyamuni Buddha. While Shakyamuni Buddha was alive, he only had about one-fifth of the power of his entirety, the great Buddha Consciousness (El Cantare Consciousness). The consciousness that the spirit of Shakyamuni Buddha belongs to is a gigantic spiritual entity that resides in the ninth dimension.

The origin of this spiritual entity can be traced back to very ancient times; it is the oldest spirit on planet Earth. One of the reasons Shakyamuni Buddha has had such a powerful influence on humankind is that this spiritual entity has been engaged in the long history of Earth since its creation. Despite being the oldest spirit, he is very active; he has sent parts of his consciousness down to earth over and over again to guide humankind. This is the truth. It is also true that he has the ultimate responsibility for Earth Spirit Group. So it is not an overstatement to say that the characteristics of this spirit built the characteristics of the civilizations on Earth.

As I have already described in *The Laws of the Sun*, parts of the spiritual entity of Shakyamuni Buddha appeared on earth, for example, as Ra Mu of the Mu Empire, Thoth of the Atlantis Empire, Rient Arl Croud of the ancient Incan Empire, and Hermes in ancient Greece.

The main work of Shakyamuni Buddha is to create the Laws, so if we trace back the roots of various religions, philosophies, and ideologies that were taught on earth, we will ultimately find that Shakyamuni Buddha is at the source of them all. In other words, they are all various manifestations of what this spirit has been thinking about in heaven.

The consciousness of Shakyamuni Buddha is part of what is called El Cantare Consciousness in the ninth dimension. If we trace back to the origin of the Laws, we will find that they ultimately stemmed from El Cantare Consciousness. Shakyamuni Buddha consciousness is the great consciousness that represents the Laws that govern all of humankind.

7

The Work of Jesus Christ

Let me touch upon the topic of Jesus Christ as well. He is very well-known, so there is no need for me to explain who he is. He has indeed been active since the creation of Earth Spirit Group. The main work of Jesus is, of course, love. Love has become a universal teaching that has spread not only to Christian countries but also to other countries. This speaks for itself as to how great Jesus' power is.

Another name for the ninth dimensional consciousness of Jesus is the Agasha Consciousness. Agasha was the light of great guiding spirit who was born on earth during the final days of Atlantis. Jesus' consciousness is often called the Agasha Consciousness after him. Sometimes, Earth Spirit Group, itself, is named after this consciousness and is referred to as the "Agasha Spirit Group." A part of Jesus' spiritual entity was born as Agasha in Atlantis approximately 10,000 years ago, and about 7,000-8,000 years ago he was born as Krishna in India. Four thousand years ago, he lived in Egypt under the name Clario. He has also been giving a lot of guidance to earth from heaven in various ways.

As I said, the main work of Jesus is love. If we imagine that the Laws, which are the function of Shakyamuni Buddha, are the human body's brain and nervous system, and at the same time, the blood vessels that run throughout the body, then Jesus' work is to pump blood into those blood vessels. Shakyamuni Buddha creates the network of blood vessels, and Jesus acts as the heart, continuously pumping blood into them. Without a heart, no part of the body would function; likewise, without the work of Jesus, the members of Earth Spirit Group would fight and hate each other, and go separate ways instead of working together. Because Jesus takes on the role of a heart and pumps the blood called "love" to all humankind, people learn that they must love each other. Jesus is an embodiment of the great power that unites people and urges them to love each other. From hundreds of millions of years ago to this day, Jesus has never once stopped his work.

Also, Jesus' work of love manifests as the activities of the medical spirit group. Jesus is the head of this spirit group. It works under Jesus' guidance and is very powerful. In truth, the population of spirits that belong to the white light, or the light of love, is very large, partly because Jesus has come down to earth many times in the past to give the teachings of love. Indeed, there is a large population of spirits who practice his teachings.

The seven archangels are also working under Jesus. They originally accompanied Enlil—whom I mentioned earlier—when he brought a large number of physical beings to planet Earth. But Jesus is primarily the one who uses the seven archangels as his disciples. Their names are Michael, Gabriel, Raphael, Raguel, Sariel, Uriel, and Phanuel, who replaced Lucifel after he fell to hell.

As the leader of the archangels, Michael takes on the role of guiding and leading people; he is also granted enormous power to stop Satan and his followers from carrying out their activities. Gabriel takes the role of a messenger; he has been given specific roles in various cultures and civilizations. There is also Raphael, who is responsible for ensuring that love flows within art, and Sariel, who is the leader of the medical spirit group. It is Sariel who is working in the field of medicine, which is one of the practical teachings of Jesus; he works to cure people's diseases. In Buddhist circles, Sariel is known as Bhaisajyaguru Tathagata or the tathagata of medicine. Also, in recent times he was born on earth as Edgar Cayce. And there is Uriel, who is mainly in charge of political matters.

8

The Work of Confucius

Aside from the two ninth dimensional spiritual entities mentioned above, there is a unique spiritual entity whose part was born as Confucius in China. As I said, he is mainly the god of learning. Learning is when knowledge of those with a higher awareness is handed down to those with a lower awareness. In fact, learning is one expression of order, which implies that the spiritual entity of Confucius, in principle, teaches order. Maintaining order is one way of bringing about harmony. I said that humans undergo soul training based on two major objectives—progress and harmony. Order is particularly important for bringing about harmony.

There is a relationship between the ruler and the ruled, or the authority and the subordinate. However, Confucius has been focused on creating an order that accords with Buddha's Will, where those closer to Buddha stand above those who are not. In other words, Confucius' main concern is how to create a well-ordered world through academic studies or the path of virtue; his focus is on how to create an orderly world where people live with Buddha's Will as their own.

To sum up, there is Shakyamuni Buddha who takes charge of the chain of command as the brain and fulfills the role of creating a network of blood vessels throughout the human body. Then there is Jesus, who plays the role of pumping blood throughout the whole body. And then the role of Confucius is to create order and maintain a balanced hierarchy. This is how they work. When we look at the long history of humankind, it is true to say that Confucius has contributed to creating highly orderly societies. The heavenly world is also an orderly world where there are spirits in higher stages and those that are not; Confucius played an extremely important role in creating this structure.

9

The Work of Moses

In the previous sections, I explained the work of Shakyamuni Buddha, Jesus, and Confucius. There is also another famous spirit—Moses, who led the Israelites out of Egypt. In terms of spiritual grade, Moses is at about the same level as Jesus and Confucius and is mainly responsible for performing miracles.

Many methods have been proposed and used to tell people about the power of Buddha, and one way is to have people feel the presence of Buddha through miracles. When miraculous phenomena that are hard to believe through earthly common sense occur, people feel that Buddha's power is at work. For instance, when Moses parted the Red Sea or received light from heaven to engrave the Ten Commandments in stone, people were overawed by these astonishing miracles and felt Buddha's mighty power. So the red light is the light of miracles to help people understand God or Buddha, and it is Moses who governs this light.

At present, Shakyamuni Buddha is taking the lead in planning and creating a new civilization, new cultures, and a new age, whereas Jesus is now taking command in heaven. Confucius is currently designing a grand plan for Earth, which will bring about the evolution of humankind and set out how humankind and Earth should be in the universe. Then, what is Moses doing? Moses is responsible for the dissolution of hell, which was formed over a history of more than 100 million years.

10

Into the World of Planetary Consciousnesses

As we have seen, the ten guiding spirits carry out their work mainly in the ninth dimension. So where does this light, which is split into seven colors in the ninth dimension, come from? It comes from the world of the tenth dimension. The tenth dimension is the realm of the spirits called the "planetary consciousnesses." Up until the ninth dimension, the spirits have the characteristics of a human spirit but the spirits in the tenth dimension are not human spirits. They have never been born as a human on earth.

There are three planetary consciousnesses in Earth's tenth dimension. First, there is Grand Sun Consciousness, which governs the positive aspect and promotes evolution on Earth. Next comes Moon Consciousness, which governs Earth's elegance, artistic beauty, grace, and its passive aspect. The active aspect (yang) governed by Grand Sun Consciousness and the passive aspect (yin) governed by Moon Consciousness have combined to make up the dualistic world on Earth. The passive elements, which would not exist in an active world, exist on Earth because of the influence of Moon Consciousness. That is to say, there is femininity in contrast to masculinity, shade in contrast to light, night in contrast to day, and the sea in contrast to mountains. Moon Consciousness is the one mainly in charge of these gentle sides of Earth.

Finally, there is Earth Consciousness, which has nurtured the planet Earth and provided energy to all the creatures living on it for the past 4.6 billion years. Earth Consciousness is the spiritual entity of planet Earth, itself, and it is within this spiritual entity that all things live. Earth Consciousness has carried out concrete activities, including the formation of mountains, the eruption of volcanoes, continental drift, movement in the Earth's crust, the flourishing of plants, and the nurturing of animals.

The three planetary consciousnesses have nurtured planet Earth over a long period of time and have had a significant influence on it.

Now, what is above the tenth dimension? It is the eleventh dimension or the world of the solar system. The consciousness of the sun, which is a stellar consciousness, exists in this eleventh dimension. Above it exists the galactic consciousness of the twelfth dimension, and in the thirteenth dimension—which is yet a grander universe beyond galaxies—exists the consciousness of the Great Universe. The multi-dimensional world extends on and on in this way until, ultimately, it reaches the world of the great Primordial Buddha, which is beyond human comprehension.

Thus, humans are walking on the road to infinite evolution with infinite levels to reach and, in the process, trying to realize progress and harmony. This is the truth about the world that surrounds humankind, the guideposts by which humankind should live, and the purpose of humankind.

Throughout all six chapters of this book, *The Laws of Eternity*, I have mainly described the worlds from the fourth dimension to the ninth dimension. This is the reality of how the world is structured. There is more than this third dimensional world and there, human beings will continue to live as a spirit, which is their true nature.

It is my earnest hope that you will base your life on this knowledge of the Truth, make it your courage to live by, and open up your path to a greater life.

Afterword

Ever since the first edition of this book was published 10 years ago, Happy Science has achieved remarkable and miraculous growth. I believe that the driving force behind our rapid growth as a religion is the grand scale of the Laws that I teach. This grand scale proves that this is a book of Truth and that what is written inside has been sent down from the Absolute Truth (true thusness). At the same time, it also proves that I, as the author conveying these Laws, am the embodiment of the Truth.

The fact that this book is truly the Laws of Eternity will eventually be proven true by how widely Buddha's Truth taught by Happy Science is accepted and how far into the future people pass it on.

People who have opened their spiritual eyes will understand that the teachings written in these pages can only be preached by the one who is the origin of the ninth dimension. If we think of the enlightenment of Zen Buddhism as the size of an artificial hill in the backyard of a home, then the enlightenment taught in this book stands well above Mount Everest. *The Laws of Eternity* is a secret treasure for humankind and the greatest mercy that El Cantare sends as a gift to humanity of this age.

Ryuho Okawa
Master & CEO of Happy Science Group
July, 1997

ABOUT THE AUTHOR

Founder and CEO of Happy Science Group.

Ryuho Okawa was born on July 7th 1956, in Tokushima, Japan. After graduating from the University of Tokyo with a law degree, he joined a Tokyo-based trading house. While working at its New York headquarters, he studied international finance at the Graduate Center of the City University of New York. In 1981, he attained Great Enlightenment and became aware that he is El Cantare with a mission to bring salvation to all humankind.

In 1986, he established Happy Science. It now has members in 169 countries across the world, with more than 700 branches and temples as well as 10,000 missionary houses around the world.

He has given over 3,500 lectures (of which more than 150 are in English) and published over 3,150 books (of which more than 600 are Spiritual Interview Series), many of which are translated into 42 languages. Along with *The Laws of the Sun* and *The Laws of Hell*, many of the books have become best sellers or million sellers. To date, Happy Science has produced 27 movies under his supervision. He has given the original story and concept and is also the Executive Producer. He has also composed music and written lyrics for over 450 pieces.

Moreover, he is the Founder of Happy Science University and Happy Science Academy (Junior and Senior High School), Founder and President of the Happiness Realization Party, Founder and Honorary Headmaster of Happy Science Institute of Government and Management, Founder of IRH Press Co., Ltd., and the Chairperson of NEW STAR PRODUCTION Co., Ltd. and ARI Production Co., Ltd.

BOOKS BY RYUHO OKAWA

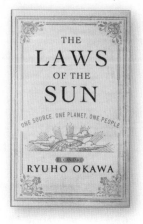

The Laws of the Sun

One Source, One Planet, One People

Paperback • 288 pages • $15.95
ISBN: 978-1-942125-43-3 (Oct. 25, 2018)

IMAGINE IF YOU COULD ASK GOD why He created this world and what spiritual laws He used to shape us—and everything around us. The truth behind the creation of the universe is revealed in this book. If we could understand His designs and intentions, we could discover what our goals in life should be and whether our actions move us closer to those goals or farther away.

At a young age, a spiritual calling prompted Ryuho Okawa to outline what he innately understood to be universal truths for all humankind. Ryuho Okawa outlines these laws of the universe and provides a road map for living one's life with greater purpose and meaning.

In this powerful book, Ryuho Okawa reveals the transcendent nature of consciousness and the secrets of our multidimensional universe and our place in it. By understanding the different stages of love and following the Buddhist Eightfold Path, he believes we can speed up our eternal process of development. The Laws of the Sun shows the way to realize true happiness—a happiness that continues from this world through the other.

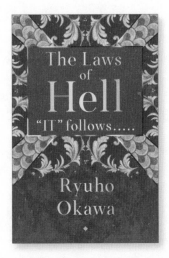

The Laws of Hell

"IT" follows.....

Paperback • 264 pages • $17.95
ISBN: 978-1-958655-04-7 (May 1, 2023)

Whether you believe it or not, the Spirit World and hell do exist. Currently, the Earth's population has exceeded 8 billion, and unfortunately, 1 in 2 people are falling to hell.

This book is a must-read at a time like this since more and more people are unknowingly heading to hell; the truth is, new areas of hell are being created, such as 'internet hell' and 'hell on earth.' Also, due to the widespread materialism, there is a sharp rise in the earthbound spirits wandering around Earth because they have no clue about the Spirit World.

To stop hell from spreading and to save the souls of all human beings, Ryuho Okawa has compiled vital teachings in this book. This publication marks his 3,100th book and is the one and only comprehensive Truth about the modern hell.

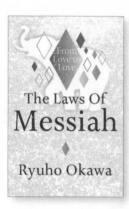

The Laws Of Messiah

From Love to Love

Paperback • 248 pages • $16.95
ISBN: 978-1-942125-90-7 (Jan. 31, 2022)

"What is Messiah?" This book carries an important message of love and guidance to people living now from the Modern-Day Messiah or the Modern-Day Savior. It also reveals the secret of Shambhala, the spiritual center of Earth, as well as the truth that this spiritual center is currently in danger of perishing and what we can do to protect this sacred place. Discover the true love of God and the ideal practice of faith, here, in this book.

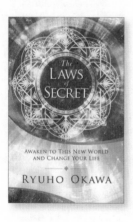

The Laws of Secret

Awaken to This New World
and Change Your Life

Paperback • 248 pages • $16.95
ISBN:978-1-942125-81-5 (Apr. 20, 2021)

Our physical world coexists with the multi-dimensional Spirit World and we are constantly interacting with some kind of spiritual energy without realizing it. This book reveals how our lives are affected by invisible influences, including the spiritual reasons behind the infection of flu, coronavirus, and other illnesses. This new view of the world will surely inspire you to become someone who can give hope and courage to others in this age of confusion.

Other Books

An Unshakable Mind
How to Overcome Life's Difficulties

Paperback • 180 pages • $17.95
ISBN:978-1-942125-91-4 (Nov. 30, 2023)

This book will guide you to build the genuine self-confidence necessary to shape a resilient character and withstand life's turbulence. Author Ryuho Okawa breaks down the cause of life's difficulties and provides solutions to overcome them from the spiritual viewpoint of life based on the laws of the mind.

The Strong Mind
The Art of Building the Inner Strength to Overcome Life's Difficulties

Paperback • 192 pages • $15.95
ISBN: 978-1-942125-36-5 (May 25, 2018)

The Strong Mind is what we need to rise time and again and to move forward no matter what difficulties we face in life. This book will inspire and empower you to take courage, cultivate yourself, and achieve resilience and hardiness so that you can break through your limits and keep winning in the battle of your life.

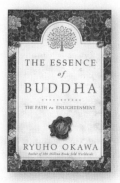

The Essence of Buddha
The Path to Enlightenment

Paperback • 208 pages • $14.95
ISBN: 978-1-942125-06-8 (Oct. 1, 2016)

The essence of Shakyamuni Buddha's original teachings of the mind are explained in simple language: how to attain inner happiness, the wisdom to conquer ego, and the path to enlightenment for people in the contemporary era. It is a way of life that anyone can practice to achieve lifelong self-growth.

The Truth about Spiritual Phenomena
Life's Q&A with El Cantare

Paperback • 232 pages • $17.95
ISBN: 978-1-958655-0-92 (Oct. 27, 2023)

These are the records of Ryuho Okawa's answers to 26 questions related to spiritual phenomena and mental health, which were conducted live during his early public lectures with the audience. With his great spiritual ability, he revealed the unknown spiritual Truth behind the spiritual phenomena.

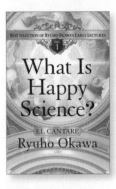

What Is Happy Science?
Best Selection of Ryuho Okawa's Early Lectures (Volume 1)

Paperback • 256 pages • $17.95
ISBN: 978-1-942125-99-0 (Aug. 25, 2023)

The Best Selection series is a collection of Ryuho Okawa's passionate lectures from the ages of 32 to 33 that reveal the mission and goal of Happy Science. This book contains the eternal Truth, including the meaning of life, the secret of the mind, the true meaning of love, the mystery of the universe, and how to end hatred and world conflicts.

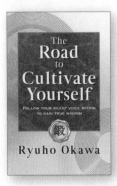

The Road to Cultivate Yourself
Follow Your Silent Voice Within to Gain True Wisdom

Paperback • 200 pages • $17.95
ISBN: 978-1-958655-05-4 (Jun. 22, 2023)

In the age of uncertainty, how should we live our lives?

This book offers unchanging Truth in the ever-changing world, such as the secrets to become more aware of the spiritual self and how to increase intellectual productivity amidst the rapid changes of the modern age. It is packed with Ryuho Okawa's crystallized wisdom of life.

The True Eightfold Path

Guideposts for Self-Innovation

Paperback • 256 pages • $16.95
ISBN: 978-1-942125-80-8 (Mar. 30, 2021)

This book explains how we can apply the Eightfold Path, one of the main pillars of Shakyamuni Buddha's teachings, as everyday guideposts in the modern-age to achieve self-innovation to live better and make positive changes in these uncertain times.

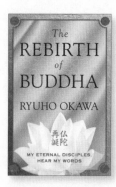

The Rebirth of Buddha

My Eternal Disciples, Hear My Words

Paperback • 280 pages • $17.95
ISBN: 978-1-942125-95-2 (Jul. 15, 2022)

These are the messages of Buddha who has returned to this modern age as promised to his eternal beloved disciples. They are in simple words and poetic style, yet contain profound messages. Once you start reading these passages, you will remember why you chose to be born in the same era as Buddha. Listen to the voices of your Eternal Master and awaken to your calling.

The Challenge of Enlightenment

Now, Here, the New Dharma Wheel Turns

Paperback • 380 pages • $17.95
ISBN: 978-1-942125-92-1 (Dec. 20, 2022)

Buddha's teachings, a reflection of his eternal wisdom, are like a bamboo pole used to change the course of your boat in the rapid stream of the great river called life. By reading this book, your mind becomes clearer, learns to savor inner peace, and it will empower you to make profound life improvements.

Words of Wisdom Series

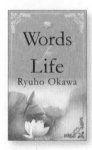

Words for Life

Paperback • 136 pages • $15.95
ISBN: 979-8-88737-089-7 (Mar. 16, 2023)

Ryuho Okawa has written over 3,150 books on various topics. To help readers find the teachings that are beneficial for them out of the extensive teachings, the author has written 100 phrases and put them together. Inside you will find words of wisdom that will help you improve your mindset and lead you to live a meaningful and happy life.

Words for Building Character

Paperback • 140 pages • $15.95
ISBN: 979-8-88737-091-0 (Jun. 21, 2023)

When your life comes to an end, what you can bring with you to the other world is your enlightenment, in other words, the character that you build in this lifetime. If you can read, relish, and truly understand the meaning of these religious phrases, you will be able to attain happiness that transcends this world and the next.

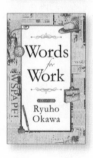

Words for Work

Paperback • 140 pages • $15.95
ISBN: 979-8-88737-090-3 (Jul. 20, 2023)

Through his personal experiences at work, Okawa has created these phrases regarding philosophies and practical wisdom about work. This book will be of great use to you throughout your career. Every day you can contemplate and gain tips on how to better your work as well as deepen your insight into company management.

Words to Read in Times of Illness

Hardcover • 136 pages • $17.95
ISBN: 978-1-958655-07-8 (Sep. 15, 2023)

Ryuho Okawa has written 100 Healing Messages to comfort the souls of those going through any illness. When we are ill, it is an ideal time for us to contemplate recent and past events, as well as our relationship with the people around us. It is a chance for us to take inventory of our emotions and thoughts.

El Cantare Ryuho Okawa Original Songs

A song celebrating Lord God / With Savior

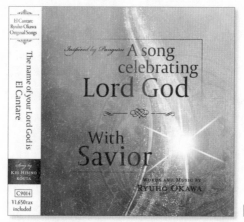

Words & Music by Ryuho Okawa

1. A song celebrating Lord God—Renewal ver.
2. With Savior —Renewal ver.
3. A song celebrating Lord God— Renewal ver. (Instrumental)
4. With Savior —Renewal ver. (Instrumental)
5. With Savior —Renewal ver. (Instrumental with chorus)

WHO IS EL CANTARE?

El Cantare means "the Light of the Earth." He is the Supreme God of the Earth who has been guiding humankind since the beginning of Genesis, and He is the Creator of the universe. He is whom Jesus called Father and Muhammad called Allah, and is *Ame-no-Mioya-Gami*, Japanese Father God. Different parts of El Cantare's core consciousness have descended to Earth in the past, once as Alpha and another as Elohim. His branch spirits, such as Shakyamuni Buddha and Hermes, have descended to Earth many times and helped to flourish many civilizations. To unite various religions and to integrate various fields of study in order to build a new civilization on Earth, a part of the core consciousness has descended to Earth as Master Ryuho Okawa.

Alpha is a part of the core consciousness of El Cantare who descended to Earth around 330 million years ago. Alpha preached Earth's Truths to harmonize and unify Earth-born humans and space people who came from other planets.

Elohim is a part of the core consciousness of El Cantare who descended to Earth around 150 million years ago. He gave wisdom, mainly on the differences between light and darkness, good and evil.

Ame-no-Mioya-Gami (Japanese Father God) is the Creator God and the Father God who appears in the ancient literature, *Hotsuma Tsutae*. It is believed that He descended on the foothills of Mt. Fuji about 30,000 years ago and built the Fuji dynasty, which is the root of the Japanese civilization. With justice as the central pillar, Ame-no-Mioya-Gami's teachings spread to ancient civilizations of other countries in the world.

Shakyamuni Buddha was born as a prince into the Shakya clan in India around 2,600 years ago. When he was 29 years old, he renounced the world and sought enlightenment. He later attained Great Enlightenment and founded Buddhism.

Hermes is one of the 12 Olympian gods in Greek mythology, but the spiritual Truth is that he taught the teachings of love and progress around 4,300 years ago which became the origin of the current Western civilization. He is a hero who truly existed.

Ophealis was born in Greece around 6,500 years ago and was the leader who took an expedition to as far as Egypt. He is the God of miracles, prosperity, and arts, and is known as Osiris in Egyptian mythology.

Rient Arl Croud was born as a king of the ancient Incan Empire around 7,000 years ago and taught about the mysteries of the mind. In the heavenly world, he is responsible for the interactions that take place between various planets.

Thoth was an almighty leader who built the golden age of the Atlantic civilization around 12,000 years ago. In Egyptian mythology, he is known as God Thoth.

Ra Mu was a leader who built the golden age of the civilization of Mu around 17,000 years ago. As a religious leader and a politician, he ruled by uniting religion and politics.

ABOUT HAPPY SCIENCE

Happy Science is a religious group founded on the faith in El Cantare who is the God of the Earth, and the Creator of the universe. The essence of human beings is the soul that was created by God, and we all are children of God. God is our true parent, so in our souls we have a fundamental desire to "believe in God, love God, and get closer to God." And, we can get closer to God by living with God's Will as our own. In Happy Science, we call this the "Exploration of Right Mind." More specifically, it means to practice the Fourfold Path, which consists of "Love, Wisdom, Self-Reflection, and Progress."

Love: Love means "love that gives," or mercy. God hopes for the happiness of all people. Therefore, living with God's Will as our own means to start by practicing "love that gives."

Wisdom: God's love is boundless. It is important to learn various Truths in order to understand the heart of God.

Self-Reflection: Once you learn the heart of God and the difference between His mind and yours, you should strive to bring your own mind closer to the mind of God—that process is called self-reflection. Self-reflection also includes meditation and prayer.

Progress: Since God hopes for the happiness of all people, you should also make progress in your love, and make an effort to realize utopia in which everyone in your society, country, and eventually all humankind can become happy.

As we practice this Fourfold Path, our souls will advance toward God step by step. That is when we can attain real happiness—our souls' desire to get closer to God comes true.

In Happy Science, we conduct activities to make ourselves happy through belief in Lord El Cantare, and to spread this faith to the world and bring happiness to all. We welcome you to join our activities!

We hold events and activities to help you practice the Fourfold Path at our branches, temples, missionary centers and missionary houses

Love: We hold various volunteering activities. Our members conduct missionary work together as the greatest practice of love.

Wisdom: We offer our comprehensive books collection, many of which bookstores do not have available. In addition, we give out numerous opportunities such as seminars or book clubs to learn the Truth.

Self-Reflection: We offer opportunities to polish your mind through self-reflection, meditation, and prayer. There are many cases in which members have experienced improvement in their human relationships by changing their own minds.

Progress: We also offer seminars to enhance your power of influence. Because it is also important to do well at work to make society better, we hold seminars to improve your work and management skills.

"The True Words Spoken By Buddha"

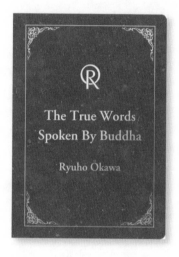

"The True Words Spoken By Buddha" is an English sutra given directly from the spirit of Shakyamuni Buddha, who is a part of Master Ryuho Okawa's subconscious. The words in this sutra are not of a mere human being but are the words of God or Buddha sent directly from the ninth dimension, which is the highest realm of the Earth's Spirit World.

"The True Words Spoken By Buddha" is an essential sutra for us to connect and live with God or Buddha's Will as our own.

MEMBERSHIPS

MEMBERSHIP

If you would like to know more about Happy Science, please consider becoming a member. Those who pledge to believe in Lord El Cantare and wish to learn more can join us.

When you become a member, you will receive the following sutras: "The True Words Spoken By Buddha," "Prayer to the Lord" and "Prayer to Guardian and Guiding Spirits."

DEVOTEE MEMBER

If you would like to learn the teachings of Happy Science and walk the path of faith, become a Devotee member who pledges devotion to the Three Treasures, which are Buddha, Dharma, and Sangha. Buddha refers to Lord El Cantare, Master Ryuho Okawa. Dharma refers to Master Ryuho Okawa's teachings. Sangha refers to Happy Science. Devoting to the Three Treasures will let your Buddha nature shine, and you will enter the path to attain true freedom of the mind.

Becoming a devotee means you become Buddha's disciple. You will discipline your mind and act to bring happiness to society.

✉ **EMAIL** OR ☎ **PHONE CALL**
Please see the contact information page.

🛜 **ONLINE** [member.happy-science.org/signup/ 🔍]

CONTACT INFORMATION

Happy Science is a worldwide organization with branches and temples around the globe. For a comprehensive list, visit the worldwide directory at happy-science.org. The following are some of our main Happy Science locations:

UNITED STATES AND CANADA

New York
79 Franklin St., New York, NY 10013, USA
Phone: 1-212-343-7972
Fax: 1-212-343-7973
Email: ny@happy-science.org
Website: happyscience-usa.org

New Jersey
66 Hudson St., #2R, Hoboken, NJ 07030, USA
Phone: 1-201-313-0127
Email: nj@happy-science.org
Website: happyscience-usa.org

Chicago
2300 Barrington Rd., Suite #400,
Hoffman Estates, IL 60169, USA
Phone: 1-630-937-3077
Email: chicago@happy-science.org
Website: happyscience-usa.org

Florida
5208 8th St., Zephyrhills, FL 33542, USA
Phone: 1-813-715-0000
Fax: 1-813-715-0010
Email: florida@happy-science.org
Website: happyscience-usa.org

Atlanta
1874 Piedmont Ave., NE Suite 360-C
Atlanta, GA 30324, USA
Phone: 1-404-892-7770
Email: atlanta@happy-science.org
Website: happyscience-usa.org

San Francisco
525 Clinton St.
Redwood City, CA 94062, USA
Phone & Fax: 1-650-363-2777
Email: sf@happy-science.org
Website: happyscience-usa.org

Los Angeles
1590 E. Del Mar Blvd., Pasadena,
CA 91106, USA
Phone: 1-626-395-7775
Fax: 1-626-395-7776
Email: la@happy-science.org
Website: happyscience-usa.org

Orange County
16541 Gothard St. Suite 104
Huntington Beach, CA 92647
Phone: 1-714-659-1501
Email: oc@happy-science.org
Website: happyscience-usa.org

San Diego
7841 Balboa Ave. Suite #202
San Diego, CA 92111, USA
Phone: 1-626-395-7775
Fax: 1-626-395-7776
E-mail: sandiego@happy-science.org
Website: happyscience-usa.org

Hawaii
Phone: 1-808-591-9772
Fax: 1-808-591-9776
Email: hi@happy-science.org
Website: happyscience-usa.org

Kauai
3343 Kanakolu Street, Suite 5
Lihue, HI 96766, USA
Phone: 1-808-822-7007
Fax: 1-808-822-6007
Email: kauai-hi@happy-science.org
Website: happyscience-usa.org